"Mr. Basile has captured the essence of Buffalo and the Niagara region..."

Mayor Anthony M. Masiello

The indispensable guide to Buffalo's best:

Restaurants • Nightlife • Arts
Sightseeing • and more

Francis R. Basile

BACKHOUSEPRESS

Buffalo's Best Places, by Francis R. Basile

Published by: Backhouse Press
                 PO Box 10873
                 Rochester, NY 14610

ISBN   0-9656691-1-4

Library of Congress Catalog Card Number: 99-72513

Thanks to everyone who helped in the research and production especially: Mary Jane Basile, Carol Bassett, Janet Hinkley, Paul E. Morris, Katie Papas, Bernie Steinkirchner, Rick Zurak, and Αγαπημενη μου Paraskevi.

Thanks also to the following organizations for their cooperation: Arts Council in Buffalo and Erie County, Erie County Parks Department, Greater Buffalo Convention & Visitors Bureau and New York Wine and Grape Foundation. Special thanks to the *Buffalo Beat*.

Copy Editor: Christine Basile
Cover Design & Maps: HYPE
Illustrations: Sasha Trouslot

Nightlife Chapter by Jeff Miers *Buffalo Beat* Arts Editor
Restaurant reviews by Helen Russell *Buffalo Beat* Dining Reviewer

ATTENTION COLLEGES, UNIVERSITIES, CORPORATIONS AND PROFESSIONAL ORGANIZATIONS:
Quantity discounts are available on bulk purchases of this book for fund raising or gift giving. For more information contact:
Backhouse Press, P.O. Box 10873, Rochester, NY, 14610; (716) 461-5585
FAX: (716) 442-3908 E-MAIL: backhousepress@juno.com

TABLE OF CONTENTS

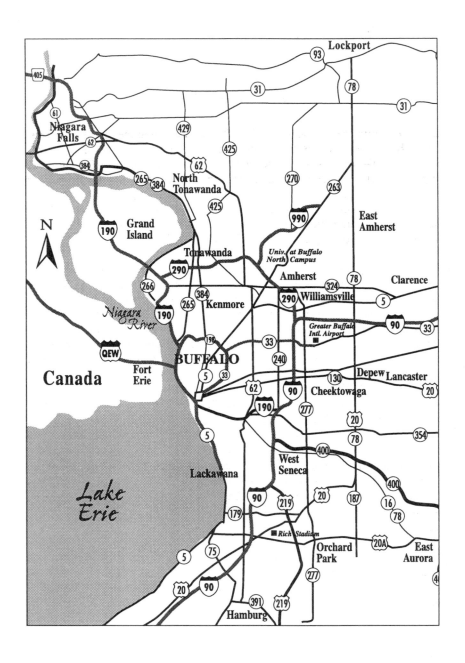

INTRODUCTION

In 1997, I published *Rochester's Best Places,* a guide to the city that sits just down the thruway from Buffalo. The success of the book led to the invariable questions of-- what will you do next? Several native and ex-Buffalonians suggested that Buffalo could use a similar book. After ignoring their advice for some time, I realized that Buffalonians are both fiercely proud and persistent. I soon began what would become a year of delving into the Queen City's history, cultural activities, and entertainment possibilities. The pages that follow chronicle my findings.

Like the Rochester book, **Buffalo's Best** was created to help the newcomer, entice the tourist, and satisfy the local resident. Although the book was designed to provide the most complete list possible of the places that represent the best of Buffalo, it is by no means an exhaustive list. (Those who feel that their favorite place was omitted or an undeserving establishment was included, are encouraged to fill out the form on page 155). **Buffalo's Best** does however, offer a look into some of the unique, mostly locally owned businesses that make the city so interesting.

The book begins with restaurant and cafe descriptions written by *Buffalo Beat* restaurant reviewer, Helen Russell. Helen spent a great deal of time tasting, writing and re-tasting, resulting in a selection of some of Buffalo's best restaurants in a wide variety of categories. The Nightlife chapter, prepared by the *Beat's* Jeff Miers (who put in some long nights of research), helps the uninitiated find the hot spots where the town parties. The rest of the book details the top sites (Exploring), the city's cultural riches (The Arts) and a number of fun activities that are available in the Niagara region (Day Trips). A calendar of annual events completes the book.

You don't need to read this book to realize that Western New York is a beautiful pace to live, work and play, but it sure helps. So the next time someone says there is nothing to do in this town, hand them a copy of **Buffalo's Best.**

I hope you enjoy using this book as much as I did writing it.

Francis R. Basile

GUIDE

The information in this book is accurate as of press time. Due to the changing nature of the retail environment, some of the information may become obsolete or inaccurate. We apologize for any inconvenience.

✉ **Addresses:** All of the addresses are located in Buffalo unless otherwise noted.
☎ **Phone Numbers:** All of the phone numbers listed use area code 716 except where noted.
☞**KIDS :** denotes activities suitable for children. For a complete listing see: *Index, Kids.*

ABOUT THE RESTAURANT CHAPTER:

The restaurant comments refer to dinner menus, food and service except where indicated. For establishments with more than one location, the first location listed is the one being reviewed, unless otherwise noted.

Restaurant pricing is classified as follows:

$	Most dinner entrees priced under $10.00.
$$	Most dinner entrees priced between $10.00 and $15.00.
$$$	Most dinner entrees priced between $15.00 and $20.00.
$$$$	Most dinner entrees priced over $20.00.

Note: The findings in this book are based on objective reporting. The restaurant reporting was always done without the knowledge of the restaurant management or staff. No complimentary meals or services were accepted.

Restaurant Reviews by Helen Russell *Buffalo Beat* Dining Reviewer
Restaurant and Cafe reviews written by the author are denoted by: frb

ATTENTION TOURISTS

For tourists or newcomers: the major sights have been matched with restaurants and/or cafes that are close to the attractions. Descriptions of establishments can be found in the appropriate chapters. Look for the ☞**NEARBY:**

Restaurants

■

RESTAURANTS BY CATEGORIES

AMERICAN-CONTEMPORARY
Audubon Room
Billy Ogden's
Calumet Arts Cafe
Cole's
Creekview Rest.
Cybele's
Dakota Grill
Daniels
Danny Ocean's
Fanny's
Fiddle Heads
Harry's Harbour Pl.
Hourglass
Hutch's
Jimmy Mac's
Left Bank
Metropolitan
Oliver's
Oscar's
Park Lane
Peabody's
Pearl Street Grill
Protocol
Sequoia
Village Pub
West End Inn
Zuzon

AMERICAN-TRADITIONAL
Country Breads
Old Orchard Inn
Old Red Mill
Roycroft Inn
Water Valley Inn

BEEF ON WECK
Cole's
Creekview
Eckl's
Schwabl's

BREAKFAST
Ambrosia
Chowbella's
Country Breads

BRUNCH
Ambrosia
Audubon Room
Left Bank
Roycroft Inn
Sequoia

CHINESE
Bamboo China
May Jen
Ming Teh

DELI
Chowbella's
Chris' NY Sand.
Mastman's Kosher
X-Cel Produce

FRENCH
Enchanté
Biac's
Rue Franklin

GERMAN
Eckl's
Schwabl's

GREEK
Ali Baba
Ambrosia

INDIAN
India Clay Oven
Tandoori

IRISH
Blackthorn

ITALIAN-NORTHERN
Il Fiorentino
Just Pasta
Little Talia
San Marco
Siena

ITALIAN-TRADITIONAL
Amici
Cambria's
Carmine's
Chef's
Chowbella's
Giacobbi's Trattoria
Italian Village
Ristor. Lombardo
Romanello's
Salvatore's

JAMAICAN
Curly's Bar & Grill

JAPANESE
Kuni's
Osaka

KOREAN
Woo Chon

KOSHER
Mastman's Kosher

MEDITERRANEAN
Ali Baba

MEXICAN
Don Pablo's

OUTSIDE DINING
Amici
Biac's
Calumet Arts Cafe
Chris' NY Sand.
Creekview Rest.
Cybele's
Enchanté
Fiddle Heads
Fritz
Harry's Harbour Pl.
Hoak's
Hutch's
Just Pasta
Left Bank
Metropolitan
Peabody's
Ristor. Lombardo
Rue Franklin
Sequoia
Siena

PACIFIC RIM
Fritz Bistro

PIZZA (SIT DOWN)
Amici
Carmine's
Giacobbi
Little Talia
Metropolitan
Pearl Street
Siena
Zuzon

POLISH
Polish Villa II

PUERTO RICAN
Niagara Cafe

SEAFOOD
Billy Ogden's
Daniels
Danny Ocean's
Fritz Bistro
Harry's Harbour Pl.
Hoak's
Hourglass
Oscar's Inn
Protocol

STEAKS & CHOPS
Audubon
Blackthorn
Creekview
Dakota Grill
Danny Ocean's
Harry's Harbour Pl.
Hourglass
Hutch's
Old Red Mill
Oscar's
Pearl Street Grill

Protocol
Salvatore's
Sequoia
Village Pub
Zuzon

SUSHI
Kuni's
Osaka

TAKE OUT
Amici
Cambria's
Chris' NY Sand.
Creekview Rest.
Jasmine Thai
King and I
Kuni's
Mastman's Kosher
May Jen
Metropolitan
Tandoori
Village Pub

THAI
Jasmine Thai
King and I

VEGETARIAN CHOICES
Ali Baba
Cybele's
Jasmine Thai
May Jen
Ming Teh
Metropolitan
Tandoori

WINGS
Anchor Bar
Duff's

RESTAURANTS BY LOCATION

AMHERST
Audubon Room
Carmine's
Danny Ocean's
Dakota Grill
Don Pablo's
Duff's
Fanny's
India Clay Oven
Protocol
Tandoori

**BUFFALO-
ALLENTOWN**
Anchor Bar
Biac's
Cybele's
Enchanté
Fiddle Heads
Rue Franklin

**BUFFALO-
DELAWARE**
Biac's
Hutch's
Park Lane
Oliver's

**BUFFALO-
DOWNTOWN**
Calumet
Chef's
Chowbella's
Pearl Street
Rue Franklin

**BUFFALO-
EAST SIDE**
Billy Ogden's

**BUFFALO-
ELMWOOD STRIP**
Ali Baba
Ambrosia
Cole's
Jimmy Mac's
Just Pasta
Kuni's
May Jen
Metropolitan
Peabody's
Sequoia
X-Cel Produce

**BUFFALO-
HERTEL AVE.**
Little Talia
Mastman's
Ristor. Lombardo

**BUFFALO-
NORTH**
Don Pablo's
Harry's Harbour Pl.
Hourglass
Oliver's
Osaka

**BUFFALO-
SOUTH**
Blackthorn

**BUFFALO-
WEST**
Left Bank
Romanello's

CHEEKTOWAGA
Jasmine Thai
Polish Villa

CLARENCE
Fritz
Old Red Mill

EAST AMHERST
Il Fiorentino

EAST AURORA
Old Orchard Inn
Roycroft Inn

EGGERTSVILLE
Giacobbi's Trattoria

FORT ERIE
Ming Teh

HAMBURG
Daniels
Hoak's
Oscar's Inn
Water Valley Inn
West End Inn

KENMORE
Amici
Hourglass

LACKAWANNA
Curly's

SNYDER
King and I
San Marco
Siena

STRYKERVILLE
Village Pub

WATERFRONT
Harry's Harbour Pl.
Hoak's
Oscar's

WEST FALLS
Country Breads

WEST SENECA
Schwabl's

WILLIAMSVILLE
Bamboo China
Creekview
Don Pablo's
Giacobbi's
Italian Village
Woo Chon
Zuzon

RESTAURANT LISTINGS

Ali Baba Mediterranean Food Garden
1116 Elmwood Ave.
886-4000
$

Ali Baba is named after a character from the *Arabian Nights,* the collection of ancient tales that originated in the Middle East and spread to Europe. Like the stories, the cuisine of the Middle East also became far reaching and the Ali Baba restaurant shows that influence. The menu, compiled by the Saudi Arabian owner, features a combination of Lebanese, Greek and Spanish food made with healthy, fresh ingredients. Starters like gazpacho and the yogurt, garlic, cucumber and mint soup (tzasiki) are seasonal, while vegetarian chili and lentil soup, with or without chicken, are always available. Most of the appetizers, pockets, pitas and dinners include popular Mid-Eastern classics like bulghur salad (tabouli), fried chickpea and fava bean patties (falafel), chickpea, tahini, and lemon juice puree (hummus) and baba ganooj, a puree of charbroiled eggplant, tahini, garlic and lemon juice. Salads are combinations of fresh greens, feta or parmesan cheeses, pine nuts, and even falafel patties with a daily selection of dressings. Pockets include a fresh garden salad. Pitas are heartier; the gyro pita has broiled seasoned lamb and beef; and the grape leaf pita is topped with feta cheese, Greek dressing, lettuce and tomatoes. To accompany the food, try the outstanding freshly squeezed citrus fruit blends. Authentic belly dancing is performed Friday nights.

Ambrosia
467 Elmwood Ave.
881-2196
$

Ambrosia, the food of the gods, is the name given to this restaurant by its Greek owners. Open every day from 7am to 11pm, this busy mid-Elmwood spot has been popular since its inception in 1984. The interior is clean and bright, with comfortable booths and Formica-topped tables that have views of both Elmwood and Hodge Avenues. Many of Ambrosia's 150 menu items are authentically Greek and most are available any time of the day or night. Although most breakfast choices and dozens of sandwiches are American, Greek dishes such as spanakopita and a variety of gyro and souvlaki pitas are featured. Appetizers include skordalia, a puree of potatoes, garlic and oil served with beet salad; and tzatziki salad with yogurt, cucumber and garlic. Dinners include stuffed grape leaves and mousaka, as well as a few American entrees, although these have a decidedly Greek influence. Baklava and rice pudding with a hint of lemon are popular Ambrosia desserts. Greek coffee is served.

Amici Ristorante and Cafe
2516 Elmwood Ave.
Kenmore
874-0143
$

Amici is an offspring of the Italian Village Restaurants, operated by the owner's daughter and son-in law. Located in a yellow brick building adjoining a quiet residential neighborhood, its cozy, friendly interior, filled with the sounds of Italian pop music, is always full. Catering to the southern Italian taste, the menu includes most of the appetizers, pasta dishes, and entrees found at the Italian Villages, but with Amici's own sauce, the winner of a local radio station's best sauce contest for two years running. Amici has a full listing of sandwiches in half and whole sizes including steak, sausage and cappicolla, pepper and egg and salami. Amici also serves pizza. Traditional Italian desserts of tiramisu, cannoli, spumoni and Italian lemon ice are served along with caffe latte, cappuccino and espresso.

Anchor Bar
1047 Main St.
886-8920
$

Every city seems to have one place that can be called a local institution. For Buffalo, this is it. Although many claim to have invented the Buffalo style chicken wing, it seems the Anchor Bar has become the true mecca for wing worshipers from around the globe. The Anchor Bar was established in the 1930's, but according to the proprietors, it hit gold one Friday evening in 1964, when hungry friends were looking for a late night snack and co-owner Teressa Bellisssimo served them a plate of chicken wings that looked too good to go into a stockpot. The rest is history. In addition to the wings and their steadfast sidekicks celery and bleu cheese dressing, the Anchor serves a full menu of entrees that lean toward Italian dishes. It's the famous wings, however, that keep them flocking in from all over. Fans can purchase small bottles and gallon jugs of the sauce along with Anchor paraphernalia. *(See also: Nightlife)*   frb

The Audubon Room
University Inn
2401 North Forest Rd.
Getzville
636-7500
$$$

The Audubon Room is part of the University Inn and Conference Center, close to the SUNY Buffalo Amherst campus. Because of this, the restaurant's identity is somewhat absorbed into that of the hotel, but the decor is tasteful and pleasant. The cuisine is contemporary without being elitist and the food is expertly prepared and beautifully presented. The menu changes regularly and popular specials are offered frequently. Appetizers include the generous onion loaf made with layers of caramelized onions, havarti and parmesan cheeses and the marinated shrimp over northern bean salad with gazpacho sauce. Representative entrees include pan-seared salmon with a horseradish crust; herbed chicken breast wrapped in prosciutto served on a visually and texturally pleasing arborio rice cake; and ravioli stuffed with seafood, and topped with a sauce of leeks, shiitake mushrooms and lemon vodka cream. Excellent rolls with tapenades and infused oils accompany dinners.

Bamboo China
6600 Main St.
Williamsville
633-5033
$

Bamboo China is a traditional Chinese-American restaurant with predictable decor and devoted service. The menu has about a dozen appetizers and soups and scores of dinner selections. Egg and spring rolls, dumplings, ribs, pancakes, dim sum and a pu pu platter are some of the appetizers. Soups include hot and sour san shan and shark's fin. Dinner entrees cover every category with the best dozen listed as chef's suggestions, such as the Bamboo China Garden Specialty of sliced chicken and scallops with fresh asparagus and mushrooms, and the Phoenix and Dragon combination of chicken and lobster with mixed vegetables, a dish of Emperor Ch'ien-Lung.

Biac's World Bistro
581 Delaware Ave.
884-6595
$$$

Located in an elegant Italianate former residence with an interior rich with stained glass, mahogany and marble fireplaces, Biac's offers cuisine of unsurpassed excellence. Dishes are brilliantly prepared by Cordon Bleu chef Sam Reda and show the influence of his native Morocco and his French mother. The specials change daily and the menu frequently. Representative appetizers might be a pungent polenta and wild mushroom tarte with porcini Madeira sauce and shaved asiago cheese; or salmon pastrami with le puy lentil, pickled red onion, and bay leaf sauce. Entrees may include rich braised lamb shank with couscous, caramelized apples and black currants; venison with sweet apple dumplings, carrot puree and juniper berry sauce; or grilled orange roughy with asparagus risotto and gorgonzola sauce. Desserts include an assortment of imported cheeses with port cream brulee and berries, or the legendary napoleon layered with pineapple, vanilla creme patisserie and passion fruit sauce. Presentation is exquisite and service genteel.

Billy Ogden's Lovejoy Grille
1834 William St.
896-8018
$$$

Billy Ogden's is so named because of its location at the corner of Ogden and William Streets. A converted house that was never much to begin with, Billy Ogden's "decor" is a combination of broken-down 1950's chrome dinette sets and fake wood paneling. Covering the walls are old advertising memorabilia, sporting items connected to Buffalo's pre-national status days and random items such as an operating barber pole. The restaurant's main attraction is the bravura cuisine of chef Andy DiVencenzo and devotees either like the defiance of the setting or put up with it for the sake of the food. The menu is displayed in colored chalk on a huge blackboard, or scrawled on a photocopied sheet. The 20 daily specials are the main feature and the reason the crowds wait for a table. Examples include blackened catfish and shrimp over angel hair pasta, loin pork chops crusted with pistachio nuts and topped with caramelized baked apples, or a whole crispy sea bass Szechuan style. Traditional Italian pasta dishes are homemade and are about half the price of entrees. Andy cooks annually at the Superbowl and his acclaimed tenderloin of pork marinated in Jack Daniels is a James Beard Foundation winner.

Blackthorn Restaurant and Pub
2134 Seneca St.
825-9327
$$

The ethnic identity of Buffalo's large Irish population is strong and well evidenced at the Blackthorn, located in predominantly Irish South Buffalo. Here too, is the Irish warmth, gift of rhetoric and food. Named after the traditional Irish walking stick, the Blackthorn serves most of the short list of typical Irish fare, as well as an eclectic selection of Americanized dishes. Soups include barley mushroom or cheddar that is thick with potatoes. Irish smoked salmon with red onion, cucumber, capers and rye toast points is a representative appetizer. The lamb stew, in a light mint gravy with dumplings and the sauteed calves' liver with onion-bacon-sherry sauce evoke images of the Emerald Isle. The several pasta dishes appeal to other tastes, while steaks, stuffed pork chops, a Friday fish fry and prime rib on the weekends round out the menu. Hot and cold sandwiches are offered as well as a long list of domestic, imported, and micro-brewed beers.

Calumet Arts Cafe
54 West Chippewa St.
855-2220
$$$

The Calumet Arts Cafe was the first restored building of the Chippewa Street renaissance and is one of its only serious restaurants. In a handsome multi-hued brick building, the interior's black walls, wonderful Toulouse-Lautrec style murals of famous jazz artists and brilliant oil paintings make a perfect backdrop for the live music on Fridays and Saturdays. A pianist performs during dinner. The menu is eclectic, combining American, Italian and Pacific Rim cuisines. Appetizers include bruchetta, fresh soups, fried shu mai (Asian dumplings) and crab cakes. Entrees include scampi verdi, with pistachio pesto on linguine and Arctic char (trout) on spinach with goat cheese and portobello mushrooms. Nightly specials are variations of the main menu. If dining at the Calumet on weekends, be prepared to pay the cover charge and stay for the show. Summer outdoor dining is pleasant in the walled garden. *(See also: Nightlife)*

Cambria's
6354 Transit Rd.
Depew
683-8843
$$

Cambria's location, in an unassuming little strip mall, is as unremarkable as its decor, but what's lacking in ambience is compensated by the quality of the food. Soups are excellent and the long list of appetizers include the generous and popular antipasto, several preparations of clams and mussels, Italian tripe, and chicken livers sauteed with wine and mushrooms. Traditional southern Italian pastas and sauces of all varieties, are well prepared, as are favorites like lasagna, ravioli, manicotti and tortellini. The dishes which put Cambria's on the map are the excellent braciola, pork tetrazzini, cannelloni stuffed with veal and spinach and the spaghetti carbonara, with ham and an egg sauce. Other classics include the pasta with chicken livers and the potato gnocci. Cambria's is a busy place with a friendly atmosphere and good service.

Carmine's
4715 Transit Rd.
Williamsville
632-2318
$

Located just north of Eastern Hills Mall, Carmine's has a winning combination of sophistication, Italian warmth and reasonable prices. The tile-rimmed brick oven stands at the restaurant's center and food is prepared in full view of the clientele. Carmine's excellent menu has all the Italian favorites as well as a number of unusual dishes. Appetizers include artichoke fritti and Sicilian style tripe. Pizzas are baked in the brick oven, of course. Diners may create their own pasta dishes, and are guided by drawings on the menu which illustrate each type of pasta. The chef's pasta specialties include familiar dishes like lasagna, linguine with clam sauce and cannelloni, along with creative dishes like penne and greens salsicci, with sliced chicken sausage, sauteed escarole and plum tomatoes in a roasted garlic sauce. Carmine's has a good selection of both veal and chicken dishes and the braciole is especially good. Family-style dinners and an antipasto bar are featured on Thursday nights.

Chef's Restaurant

291 Seneca St.
856-9187
$

Chef's is a favorite meeting place of Buffalo politicos, judges, lawyers and police. Situated a few blocks east of downtown, the restaurant conveniently has its own enclosed, lighted parking lot across the street. One of Buffalo's best known Italian family restaurants since 1923, its two dining rooms of 56 tables, covered with red and white checked cloths, are always full. The menu is displayed on large wooden placards. Available every day are veal and chicken cacciatore as well as the usual pasta dishes. Special entrees are served on assigned days of the week. For example, eggplant parmesan is served every Monday, and chicken in white wine on alternate Tuesdays. The featured entrees on other days are braciole, veal scallopini, calamari, tripe and chicken livers, with seafood served on Fridays. Chef's spaghetti sauce is so well-liked that it is bottled and sold in local supermarkets. Two of its salads, the dandelion and the zucchini, are legendary. Italian desserts such as tortonti, spumoni, cannoli and cheesecake have been Chef's standards for years, with tiramisu a recent addition. The atmosphere is casual and comfortable and the service snappy. Chef's low prices and good food make it a real bargain.

Chowbella's

206 S. Elmwood Ave.
852-1286
Breakfast and Lunch only
$

Chowbella's, in the wonderful old brick Huron Hotel, near both downtown and Allentown, is an authentically decorated New York style deli and sandwich shop. Deli cases display meats, cheeses, quiche, lasagna along with cold salads that can be purchased by the pound; such as, the couscous and olive salad or the asiago chicken salad. Eat-in patrons sit at green-topped tables against the windows or on the balcony. Over thirty wonderful sandwiches are on the menu, each with imaginative names and ingredients. The popular Fun Guy is a grilled portobello mushroom with Swiss cheese, red onion and garlic mayo. The Papa Mia is marinated eggplant, salami, asiago cheese and artichoke spread. The Sergeant Pepper is roasted peppers, gorgonzola, romaine and sun dried tomatoes. These hefty sandwiches are made on focaccio or chibatta breads and are accompanied by a side of pasta salad. Hearty homemade soups include the pasta fagiole or changing daily specials. Espresso, cappuccino, and latte are also served. Chowbella's pies are home baked and the apple caramel is especially good. Don't miss the breakfast giabrotte, a scramble of eggs, Italian sausage, peppers, onions and potatoes.

Chris' NY Sandwich Co.
395 Delaware Ave.
854-6642
$

A handsome little shop right across the street from the Buffalo Club, Chris's NY Sandwich Company does a rousing lunchtime business with the downtime working crowd. Inside, the stylish dining room has coral-colored tables, black Milanese style chairs and a display of cacti in brightly glazed pots. Sandwich ingredients are of high quality and healthier choices are marked. Old standbys like ham, turkey, corned beef, capocollo and roast beef are offered, as well as new favorites such as chicken salad with fresh pineapple and walnuts, and smoked turkey-dill salad. From the grill there are turkey and sirloin burgers, chicken and Black Angus sirloin steak. Specialty sandwiches include grilled marinated eggplant with melted fontinella cheese, roasted red peppers and pesto and the grilled portobello mushroom with sauteed spinach, fontinella, and garlic mayo. On Fridays, baked Cajun cod fillet with dill mayo is offered. Garden, pasta and fresh fruit salads are available as sides or meals. Beverages include Stewart's orange cream soda and root beer, Boylan's red birch beer, and "smoothie" shakes of fresh fruit, yogurt and crushed ice.

Cole's
1104 Elmwood Ave.
886-1449
$$

Cole's has been a Buffalo dining and drinking establishment since 1934. The Tudor style room with its vaulted ceiling, is hung with generations of sports paraphernalia including banners from a plethora of colleges and universities, a rowing club shell and wooden placards listing the annual winners of the James E. Parker Memorial Foot Race. Primarily a popular bar where good, traditional food is served, Cole's menu is a combination of hearty sandwiches, a great selection of appetizers and several dinner entrees. Sandwiches include the Cole's club, the reuben, beef on weck, and burgers. The large selection of appetizers includes shrimp cocktail, clams on the half shell, steamers, clams casino, and soups like the famous seafood bisque. Steaks, barbecued ribs, lamb chops, grilled fish and chicken dominate the entrees over other comfortable combinations of chicken or shellfish with pasta or rice. More than the food, it's the ghosts of Buffalo's sporty aristocratic past that make Cole's one of Buffalo's more interesting eateries.

Country Breads & More
1089 David Rd. (Rte.240)
West Falls
655-0039
$

Primarily a family breakfast and lunch restaurant, Country Breads and More is situated in a country setting not far from Orchard Park. The decor is homey with warm oak, calico and lace. A large pleasant dining room was added to the original modest structure to accommodate weekend crowds. Baskets of delicious home baked breads and rolls are a big attraction. Breakfasts are hearty and wholesome, with whole grain pancakes and pure maple syrup. A wide variety of omelettes and egg dishes are featured including eggs benedict. Lunches consist of excellent salads, sandwiches on homemade breads, and quiche. Lofty pies, dumplings and cookies are popular dessert choices, and can be bought over the counter. A midday dinner is served on Saturdays and Sundays. Country

Breads does a heavy catering business for small and large affairs.

Creekview Restaurant
5629 Main St.
Williamsville
632-9373
$

Creekview's location in the center of the Village of Williamsville, on the bank of Ellicott Creek is its prime attraction, with an outdoor covered porch affording a restful view of the creek's tiny waterfall. To accommodate its lively crowd, Creekview has expanded beyond the bar, originally the only room in this old village landmark, to three dining rooms including the porch. Creekview can draw a crowd for both lunches and dinners. Hearty appetizers include oyster stew made to order, raw or steamed clams, bacon-wrapped chicken livers, and mushrooms stuffed with sausage, spinach and feta. Light meals include Caesar and spinach salads or sandwiches like the Creekview steak sandwich with mushrooms, spinach and bleu cheese. Linguine with clam sauce and penne with spinach, sundried tomatoes and leeks in a roquefort-tomato broth are two pasta offerings. Entrees tend toward broiled or fried fish, shrimp, scallops, oysters and steaks. Ambitious dinner specials are served nightly. Desserts include the terrific key lime pie.

Curly's Bar and Grill
647 Ridge Road
Lackawanna
824-9716
$$$

Curly's, established in 1934, was reinvented by the original owner's granddaughter after she graduated from the culinary Institute of America and worked at restaurants around the world. Choosing principally a Jamaican theme, she and her chef husband helped turn Curly's into one of the few bright spots in post-steel Lackawanna. Half of Curly's is a wood-paneled pub; the other half is the Jamaican room, its walls covered with brightly colored Caribbean murals. Some of the unusual appetizers include conch fritters, grilled shrimp with Caribbean salsa, and deviled clams.

Soups change daily; tomato with artichoke shows up occasionally while black bean dolloped with sour cream is always on the menu. Jamaican jerk chicken is featured several ways; as an entree, in the Caesar salad, and as a sandwich. The jerk sauce is also bottled and sold. Other Jamaican fare includes the chicken ochie, a peanut crusted chicken breast with a plum banana curry sauce; Jamaican escovitche fish with peppers onions and a spicy tomato sauce; and the blue fish fillet with a white wine cream sauce. Inexplicably, the non-Jamaican fare leans towards northern Italian. On the substantial list of pasta specialties are shellfish and shrimp in either a marinara sauce or a light blush cream sauce and Silk and Satin, a julienne of prosciutto, mushrooms, peas, basil in a white wine cream sauce. Desserts are made on premises and include; the Swiss roll, a crisp almond roll filled with Belgian chocolate mousse; and homemade ice creams, rum raisin being one example.

Cybele's
99 Elmwood Ave.
882-1247
$

Named after the ancient nature goddess, tiny Cybele's, just north of Allen Street, is retro hippie with a vengeance. Dining areas are divided into two rooms, one with an exposed kitchen, the other, an adjoining closet-sized room. There is also a patio available for outside dining. Chipped, unmatched crockery mixes with books, papers and clutter on the shelves. Also visible is the iron sink where dishes are hand washed. Huge oil paintings cover the orange walls. Tidiness is not at a premium at Cybele's. Appropriately, the music of Bob Dylan, The Beatles and Sonny and Cher plays. The bill of fare changes daily and is written on a piece of colored construction paper and passed around. Service is mellow and the food is good and right in step with today's cuisine. Examples are crepes, perfectly made and feathered-edged, either stuffed with ginger, soy, mushrooms and onions with a sweet-sour sauce, or with zucchini and onion and a creamy parmesan sauce. Quiche is du jour. Two entree possibilities are mater paneor, an Indian dish of cheese, cauliflower and green peas in a tomato-yogurt sauce served over rice; and cheddar-stuffed chicken breast with cilantro cream sauce, black beans and rice. Desserts like the rich, hearty carrot cake, heavy with nuts; and cheesecake, made on premises, are exhibited in the oak, glass-fronted ice box.

The Dakota Grill
4224 Maple Rd.
Amherst
834-6600
$$$

The Dakota Grill's motif is the unlikely combination of a Manhattan jazz club of the 30's or 40's, a roadhouse tavern and a menu with a Western U.S. spin. Located in one of Amherst's many automobile-dependent strip malls, the interior is as successfully staged as a movie set with a long handsome bar, murals depicting jazz greats, dark wood, brass fittings, green leather and crisp white linen. Some dishes that are Western by name if not by birth are the Flatirons garlic bread with Cowboy Caviar (bean dip) and the North and South Dakota, which is a sirloin steak with jambalaya. The cuts of certified Angus steaks are tender and flavorful. Non-Western dishes include the delicious appetizer of chevre cheese over portobello mushroom slices, and the delicate salmon with a chili rub. Desserts, like the all-American caramel apple pie with ice cream and the Belgian chocolate brownie filled with raspberry, ganache and pecans are sumptuous. Port and cigars are available at the cigar bar.
(See also: Nightlife)

Daniels
174 Buffalo St.
Hamburg
648-6554
$$$

One of the Southtowns' finer restaurants, Daniels, in a converted house, has about a dozen tables in an intimate and elegantly simple interior. An extensive, superb daily menu is supported by the brief regular menu. Plates are beautifully presented and service is refined. Appetizers may include crab cake with Napa cabbage-citrus slaw and red pepper aioli or porcini mushroom-crusted ostrich with apple-turnip relish and potato pancake. Offered regularly are escargot with tomatoes and garlic butter in a homemade pasta sheet. The salad of house-smoked trout with mixed greens, apples, walnuts and citrus vinaigrette is wonderful, and the roast beet salad with fresh asparagus, hard cooked egg, and field greens is unusual. Seafood choices may include halibut fillet with poppy seed crust and saffron butter on a bed of braised fennel or grilled yellowfin tuna with hoisin (soy based) glaze served with a risotto cake. A grilled certified Angus New York strip steak is often served with gorgonzola cheese, onions and potato-bell pepper hash. Saddle of venison is marinated in red wine and juniper, and served with spaetzle. The glorious duck breast with roast pear puree and raspberry sauce is regularly served, as are the medallions of veal tenderloin with slices of lobster. Deluxe desserts may include lemon tart with an almond pastry shell, bittersweet chocolate mousse with pistachio sauce or a napoleon with coconut pastry cream and sauteed bananas.

Danny Ocean's
5433 Transit Rd.
Williamsville
568-1000
$$$$

Under the same ownership as Billy Ogden's, Danny Ocean's is named after the movie which starred Frank Sinatra and his Rat Pack buddies. Sinatra is everywhere. The movie plays continuously on the VCR without sound, Sinatra and Las Vegas posters hang on the walls, and his music croons in the background. The strip mall location puts a damper on the theme, but the decor is refined nonetheless. The cuisine is bold, robust and heady; rich in flavor, with a menu that changes daily, depending on the availability of the ingredients and the whim of the chef. Possible appetizers include a simple vichyssoise or the lusty beef carpaccio, paper-thin shaved slices of uncooked filet mignon with a dijon remoulade and parmesan curls. Possible entrees are the boldly flavored veal rolatini with prosciutto, Italian sausage, and mascarpone stuffing; the musky tenderloin of pork marinated in Jack Daniel's with apples, onions, bacon and whipped yams; or the halibut filet pan-seared with jumbo scallops over asiago risotto and tomato-chive cream. Desserts of the same intensity are the chocolate-chestnut paté with espresso creme anglaise; mascarpone cheesecake and key lime chiffon tart.

Don Pablo's

1951 Elmwood Ave.
873-8731
$
also:
6727 Transit Rd.
Williamsville
633-0933
1591 Niagara Falls Blvd.
Amherst
832-8007

Buffalo is so far from our nation's southern border that any version of Mexican food is welcomed here, even one from a chain of 200 Don Pablo's out of Lubbock, Texas. The red brick building, one of their nationwide designs, is remarkably similar to the 1930's factories at this end of Elmwood Avenue. The interior has an abbreviated selection of the necessary Mexican tile, potted palms and southwestern furniture. All of the familiar Mexican dishes are represented: nachos, bean dip and guacamole, quesadillas, tortillas, chimichangas, burritos, enchiladas, tacos and flautas, individually or as part of combination platters. Dishes are made from scratch and low fat meats are cooked over genuine mesquite.

Duff's
3651 *Sheridan Dr.*
Amherst
834-6234
$

For many aficionados of Buffalo chicken wings, there's no place that can match Duff's. On the busy intersection of Sheridan and Millersport, the windowless, but bright dining room has seen more chicken than Frank Perdue. Established in 1946, Duff's began serving wings in the late 60's. Today over 5,000 pounds of chicken wings are sold each week. The popular lunch special includes 10 wings and a choice of two of the following sides: fries, salad or soup. Only the brave need to venture beyond the medium sauce, a fiery red concoction that lightly coats the wings. In addition to wings, Duff's serves sandwiches and specials.   frb

Eckl's Beef and Weck Restaurant
4936 Ellicott Rd.
Orchard Park
662-2262
$$

Owned by the Eckl family since 1906, many consider Eckl's the best source of beef on kummelweck in the area. The restaurant is housed in an 1840's structure that was moved half a block when Buffalo Road was widened in 1963. Part cozy bar and part restaurant, Eckl's serves Black Angus prime roast beef and the 35 pound steamship rounds are carved behind the bar. Eckl's uses a soft roll with salt and caraway seeds imbedded in the dough before baking. Beef on weck can be ordered individually or as a plate with a slightly sweetened homemade cole slaw and German potato salad from old family recipes. Steaks, chops and burgers are available along with prime rib on the weekends. Fin and shellfish are also well represented by the haddock, orange roughy, scallop, shrimp and oyster plates and the lobster tail dinner.

Enchanté
16 Allen St.
885-1330
$$$$

Enchanté, one of a handful of genuine French restaurants in Buffalo, has a loyal following of connoisseurs of French and Continental cuisine. Occupying the original 1829 red brick home of Dr. Allen (for whom Allen Street is named), the first floor early Victorian dining rooms are sumptuously decorated with formal wallpapers, draperies and carpets, and furnished in the Queen Anne style. A charming narrow staircase leads to the cigar bar and private dining room on the second floor. Sheltered by a canopy of leafy branches and huge umbrellas, the flagstone garden dining patio has a enchanting intimacy. The menu, written in both English and French, changes daily. Examples of appetizers include escargot, wild mushroom and spinach puff pastry with garlic cream sauce; salmon, smoked on the premises with creme fraîche; and a mussel, saffron and orange soup. Entrees read like poetry; chicken breast stuffed with white truffles, served with leek marmalade and white port truffle sauce and a medley of fish and shellfish with vegetables in a light Chardonnay cream sauce. After the entrees, a sophisticated fruit and cheese tray is presented. The selection includes such cheeses as bleu d'avergne, a blue-veined creamy roquefort-like cheese; and petit pont d'èveque, a soft cheese similar to brie. Desserts such as the light, cool mango charlotte are characteristic.

Fanny's
3500 Sheridan Road
Amherst
834-0400
$$$$

Named after 1920's celebrity Fanny Brice, Fanny's has been evoking glamour and style for over 25 years. The windowless interior is done in black and shades of brown, copper and bronze. Live jazz is performed by legendary jazz greats on Friday and Saturday nights in the striking black and white mirrored bar. French doors open into the handsome, adjoining dining room. The tables are surrounded with pillars and railings, and lush, extremely private booths are against the walls. Service is formal and professional and every plate is a work of art. Fanny's cuisine has a perfection of detail that propels each menu item, even the humblest bed of greens, to well beyond their menu description. Appetizers include grilled portobello mushrooms with balsamic vinegar, stilton cheese, and Italian olives; and escargot in garlic cream sauce with Pernod in a French baguette. Fanny's famous seafood bisque is thick with lobster, scallops and shrimp in a saffron cream base. Veal and tournado entrees change du jour. A tournado special may be with Madeira brown sauce and shiitake mushrooms. Sea bass is grilled with mango salsa; and lobster "le scoot" is sauteed, stuffed with shrimp and served in a cognac cream sauce. Fanny's sirloin pepper steak is encrusted with cracked peppercorns and sauteed with cognac and Madeira. The gorgeous desserts change daily and might include a flaky-crusted raspberry mango strudel with vanilla sauce and berries or white and dark chocolate mousse torte impaled with spears of marbleized chocolate over a caramel sauce with vanilla ice cream.

Fiddle Heads
62 Allen St.
883-4166
$$$

Fiddle Heads, at the corner of Allen and Franklin Streets in Allentown, is a small, popular, somewhat self-conscious restaurant with a reputation for intimate dining and outstanding cuisine. The building is a brick storefront with plate glass windows overlooking the passing scene and the interior is understated and minimalist. The atmosphere is rarefied and the service, coolly efficient. Attire is well-dressed casual. Several outdoor tables are available in pleasant weather. Fiddle Heads' menu has three appetizers and six or seven entrees for both lunch and dinner and changes frequently. Each menu features several selections so avant garde they are familiar only to the most up-to-date-gourmet. *Capunatina,* ricotta *crespelle,* and *caponata* may compel only the stout-hearted to ask for translations from the servers. Other entrees are more familiar, a certified Angus strip loin, with baked potato and dill sour cream or spring chicken with goat cheese mashed potatoes, served with a warm artichoke and arugula salad. The mussels in white wine, garlic butter and lemon are delicious and the shrimp cocktail with three chutneys appealing. Fiddle Heads' homemade pasta is excellent, and the thin linguine is wonderful with sauteed shrimp and sun-dried tomato. Fiddle Heads' popularity requires reservations well in advance.

Fritz American Bistro
6010 Goodrich Rd.
Clarence Center
741-5085
$$$

A trendy newcomer, Fritz occupies a tiny storefront in the charming crossroad hamlet of Clarence Center. The decor is high Eurostyle, with polished blonde wood, eggshell walls and nary a soft surface to alleviate sound or rest the eye. Packed into the main dining room, with its diminutive central bar, and small adjoining dining room, are about 18 tables. The server to diner ratio is high and the staff pleasant, although the etiquette is sometimes lacking. Paradoxically, this "American Bistro" features, almost exclusively, cuisine from the Pacific Rim, with a strong emphasis on seafood. Appetizers might be a ginger-carrot based soup with shrimp and sea bass; giant scallops in coconut curry cream over potato pancakes; or Thai marinated beef over sesame rice noodles. Entrees include sea bass dipped in sake and sauteed with vegetables; stir-fried shrimp with cabbage served over Japanese noodles; or lemon grass dusted salmon with ginger vinaigrette served over sweet Korean wild rice. Even the desserts express the Asian influence. Some choices include a pear tart with caramel sauce; ginger creme brulee with fresh berries; or tiramisu with lychee and strawberries.

Giacobbi's Trattoria
3945 Main St.
Eggertsville
836-4422
$

Giacobbi's Trattoria is a comfortable, family-style restaurant in a small, tasteful mall on the corner of Eggert Road and Main Street. The larger of the two dining rooms has a glazed-tile wood-fired brick oven in which gourmet pizzas, such as the primavera with fresh vegetables and pesto are baked. Adjoining the smaller dining room is a cozy greenhouse. In true trattoria fashion, all entrees can be ordered family-style, making Giacobbi's excellent fare at a very reasonable price. The many appetizers include an abundant antipasto, Sicilian style hot peppers and wonderful artichoke fritters served with a spinach-gorgonzola sauce. The crab and shrimp bisque is a *Taste of Buffalo* award winner. Pasta entrees include frutti di mare, an assortment of seafood over linguine with a choice of oil and garlic or marinara sauce; and fettucine with grilled chicken breast and fresh vegetables served in a light pesto cream sauce. The pasta rotolo is stuffed with grilled eggplant, portobello mushrooms, roasted red peppers and goat cheese. Among the entrees is another *Taste of Buffalo* award winner, the grilled scallops wrapped with prosciutto and served over grilled vegetables with red and yellow pepper sauces. The sauteed veal medallions with spinach, mushroom and roasted red peppers in a light demi glaze with goat cheese is unsurpassed. Simple Italian desserts round out the meal.

Harry's Harbour Place Grille
2192 Niagara St.
874-5400
$$$

Located on the Niagara River overlooking Strawberry Island, Harry's Harbour Place is designed with randomly shaped rooms that easily flow into each other, affording every table a view of the river. The muted greys and tans of the decor underplay rather than compete with the riverside setting. Terraces on the river and marina sides of the sand-colored stucco structure allow outdoor dining and lounging in fair weather. The atmosphere is relaxed and somewhat casual. The seafood portion of Harry's menu shares equal billing with steaks, chops and chicken. Harry's rich signature chowder of whole baby clams, scallops and other seafood in a cream stock is the leading appetizer. Close behind is the broiled, crusted, gratineed escargot; clams casino; oysters Rockefeller; excellent seafood cakes with Cajun remoulade; and smoked salmon with gorgonzola croquette. Seafood entrees include broiled and grilled sea scallops, salmon, and swordfish; and a mixed seafood grill. The stew of mussels, little neck clams, scallops and salmon is simmered in a roasted garlic and asiago cream sauce. Some desserts are tiramisu and New York style cheesecake.

Hoak's Lakeshore Restaurant
4100 Lakeshore Rd.
Hamburg
627-7988
$

Buffalonians still associate seafood with lakeshore restaurants, even though the fruit of Lake Erie ceased to be served there over a half century ago. Hoak's Lakeshore Restaurant has hugged Lake Erie's shore since 1949. The dining rooms are homey and comfortable and afford a lake view. The outdoor deck overlooking the water becomes a dining room in the summer. Appetizers include shrimp and clams prepared several ways and fresh New England and Manhattan clam chowder. Broiled shrimp, scallops, crab legs, and lobster tail are served simply with salad and potato. Non-seafood offerings include roast beef, pork chops, barbecued ribs, an array of steaks, surf and turf, and several preparations of chicken. Beef on weck, steak and fish sandwiches, burgers and specialty sandwiches round out the menu.

The Hourglass Restaurant

981 Kenmore Ave.
877-8788
$$$

Under the same ownership for over 30 years and with the same chef for nearly 20, The Hourglass is one of the area's finest restaurants. The interior is softly quiet in color and although the atmosphere is cordial and formal, it has a warm and easy grace. Owner Terry Bechakas, a charming and elegant host, personally seats all patrons. The exemplary wait staff practices every serving refinement, from placing the open menu in guests' hands to providing every proper utensil. Seafood, a major focus, is uncompromisingly fresh and knowledgeably selected. Appetizers include little neck clams; smoked salmon; trout and bluefish with horseradish whipped cream; and poached haddie with mornay sauce. Some main courses include sole with snow crab and mushroom stuffing wrapped in puff pastry; angel hair pasta tossed with mussels and chicken; braised pheasant with pink and green peppercorns; and a pound and a half lobster, broiled, steamed or stuffed with shrimp. Era Bechakas' extraordinary homemade desserts change nightly and may include: dark chocolate raspberry cheesecake; blackberry cobbler with homemade peach ice cream; and lemon tart with paper-thin lemon slices, blueberry sauce and homemade vanilla ice cream. The Hourglass wine cellar is exceptional and the wine list extensive, with several renowned bottles available, many of which are unlisted.

Hutch's

1375 Delaware Ave.
885-0074
$$$

The building in which Hutch's is located was allegedly once a livery stable. Its low ceilings, bentwood chairs, noisy atmosphere and crooked rooms give it a bistro-like atmosphere. The adjoining bar is decorated with marvelous French and American posters from the 1940's and 50's. Hutch's excellent appetizers and entrees change daily and are presented verbally as a long list of specials. Although menu choices are not particularly unusual, the ingredients are of the highest quality and are prepared with talented expertise and great creative flair. Appetizers such as soft-shell crab with field greens or saffron risotto with fresh crab and scallops are offered. Lamb chops, black Angus beef, chicken, a good selection of fish including a nightly salmon special are featured. Special entrees may include; halibut with spinach almond pesto, marinated and grilled Cornish game hen with potato pancakes, and lamb chops with roasted garlic demiglaze. Hutch's caters to the whims of the chic urban crowd by offering appealing small plates for under $10, such as a half rack of ribs, grilled vegetable quesadillas, pan-fried Maryland oysters with Cajun remoulade, and mussels scampi. Desserts are sumptuous and excellent. Attire is upscale casual to dressy, the service exceptionally professional and the atmosphere lively.

Il Fiorentino

8485 Transit Rd.
East Amherst
625-4250
$$$$

Chef GianCarlo Bruni met his wife, Sandra, at his restaurant outside of Florence while she was studying design in Italy. When they opened a restaurant off of Kenmore Avenue in Buffalo they named it after their beloved city. They've now relocated to East Amherst and the new restaurant captures the country atmosphere of the original restaurant in the Tuscan hills. It's beautifully designed with dark rich oak wainscoting and walls hung with antique etchings of notable Italian sites. Il Fiorentino is comfortable and cultured with Italian opera as the musical background. The menu has not been tempered to suit American taste, but remains true to its roots. The food is wonderfully rich, with flavors fully developed. Pasta and risotto can be served as appetizers in half portions or as full, second courses. Examples are pasta carrettiera, with Parma ham, tomatoes and olives; or risotto with scallops and saffron. Sauces are superb. Dinner courses might include a pork tenderloin in a red wine sauce, tender game hen, or grilled trout with rosemary and lemon. Desserts include creme brulee, biscotti and the classic cream puff with chocolate sauce. A retail shop of specialty foods and wines from Italy adjoins the restaurant.

India Clay Oven

940 Millersport Hwy.
Amherst
832-1030
$

The India Clay Oven is small, understated and a bit hard to find. Owned by native Indians, the food is faithful to the national fare, with most dishes on the menu written in both Indian and English. Meals start with papadum or cumin-flavored lentil chips. Many appetizers consist of deep fried flour shells, stuffed or not, or deep fried potatoes or vegetable fritters. The ten varieties of bread include pan fried, deep fried, baked, layered or stuffed with cheese, potatoes, onions or lamb. Biryani is aromatic rice with nuts and raisins to which is added vegetables, chicken, beef, lamb, shrimp or a combination thereof. Entrees consist of these meats cooked in a curry sauce or with combinations of vegetables and spices often served with a yogurt sauce. The long list of vegetarian entrees combine vegetables and legumes with garlic, ginger, cheese and flavorful sauces. A wonderful mango chutney can be ordered on the side. Dessert is authentic rice pudding.

Italian Village Restaurant

804 Wehrle Dr.
Williamsville
634-1804
$$

This restaurant, one of two Italian Villages, has an unimposing exterior and a comfortable interior given to whites, creams and mirrors. A full range of southern Italian dishes of extremely high quality are served. Clams casino is frequently available, as is an excellent bruschetta. Pasta fagiole, homemade lentil and tortellini soups and a well-stocked antipasto are some menu choices. The exceptional homemade pasta

also:
313 Grant St.
886-8285

and bright red, sweet sauce contribute to the high quality of the baked pasta dishes like lasagna and manicotti. A choice of pasta can be topped with any of thirteen sauces including; marinara, shrimp fra diavolo, garlic and oil or shrimp scampi. Some of the specialty pasta dishes include: linguine carbonara with cream sauce, ham, cheese and egg; linguine cartiera, with black olives, anchovies and garlic; and tortellini with peas and meat sauce. Some of the several popular ways that veal or chicken is served are: Marsala, with mushrooms and marsala wine; Francese, in a light lemon sauce; Margharita, with wine, eggplant, ham and mozzarella; and Milanese, breaded and baked with lemon. A number of "American style" entrees are also available. From the dessert tray, the overstuffed cannoli with homemade shells and filling are exceptional.

Jasmine Thai II
3719 Union Rd.
Cheektowaga
683-6553
$$

Jasmine Thai II, has a tiny bar in front of two cozy dining rooms. The rooms are decorated with large fabric wall hangings worked with gold thread depicting an elephant, the traditional symbol of Thailand. Appetizers include egg and spring rolls, dumplings, delicious deep fried and creamy-centered crab ragoon with two cheeses, and steamed mussels. Two interesting soups are hot and sour shrimp and the chicken coconut with coconut milk and lime. Yum, a sort of vegetable, fruit and meat salad, includes nam sod yum, ground pork with fresh ginger. Curries, like many Thai dishes, are spicy and prepared with curry paste and perhaps coconut milk or peanuts. Seafood, chicken, pork, or beef are sauteed with vegetables, nuts, or pineapple, and in some cases, curry or ginger paste. Chef's specialties are the Pataya Chicken with broccoli and peanut sauce; Imperial Pork with green curry and eggplant; Siam Duck with cashews and pineapple; and the spicy Seafood Paradise of mixed seafood with a chili and herb sauce. Vegetarian, noodle, and fried rice dishes are numerous. A tasty dessert is coconut ice cream topped with honey, sesame seeds and "coins" of deep fried, eggroll skin-wrapped banana slices.

Jimmy Mac's
555 Elmwood Ave.
886-9112
$

Jimmy Mac's, a mid-Elmwood Avenue institution is equal portions yuppie bar and easy going restaurant. The dark and moody corner bar was expanded by adding a neon-lit atrium on the Anderson Place side with about a dozen tables where light lunches and dinners are served. The menu has more wit than substance, with pasta, pizza, salad, burgers, and sandwiches familiar to most. Starters include soups; potato skins; Greek, julienne and Caesar salads; and wings. Grilled ribs, steaks and chops are served. Three or four pricier dinner specials are offered nightly. The stylish atrium resounds with bar noise and can be chilly in the winter. Service is perky.

Just Pasta
307 Bryant St.
881-1888
$$$

Just Pasta is a well-established restaurant a block from the Elmwood Strip in an attractive brick building on the corner of Ashland. Its elegantly decorated interior features restored murals created decades ago for the legendary, now defunct, Leonardo's Grotto Bar downtown. Seating is at intimate tables or comfortable booths with white linen and fine glassware. Patio dining is popular when the weather is cooperative and particularly pleasant on the quieter side street. Changing exhibits of local artwork are featured complete with opening nights to introduce the artists. As for the food, Just Pasta's menu has been one of the city's best for a number of years. Its imaginative pasta offerings are well-balanced with contemporary entrees. A recent example of a pasta dish is the gulf shrimp, prosciutto cotta, tomatoes, basil and peas with lemon fettucine. A typical entree could be the grilled, spice rubbed pork chops with summer peach barbeque and smashed potatoes. Appetizers and salads are created with the same integrity, and the desserts, displayed temptingly at the front entrance, are almost impossible to resist and have long been the subject of Buffalo culinary conversation. Lunches and dinners are treated with equal attention, and a late night dessert at Just Pasta is unsurpassed.

King and I
3933 Harlem Rd.
Eggertsville
839-2950
$

This bright, fresh storefront is decorated with memorabilia from the owner's native Bangkok. Warm service accompanies sonorous, melodic Thai music. Thai food is spicy, and rice, coconut and coconut milk are staples. King and I appetizers include chicken satay, a Thai shish kabob of grilled chicken marinated in spiced coconut cream served with peanut sauce and sweet cucumber salad. Two great soups are tom kha, a sweet coconut soup; and poh tak, a very spicy seafood soup with lemon grass. Curries and stir fries are features. House specialties include poh heang, a spicy steamed mix of scallops, shrimp, and squid, served bubbling hot in an earthenware pot; and the milder ped gra pow, roasted duck with vegetables and pineapple in a basil chive sauce. Pla prew wan is a magnificent fried whole fish topped with vegetables and pineapples in a sweet and sour sauce. Rice pudding made with coconut milk and topped with bright yellow sweet custard makes a tasty finish.

Kuni's
752 Elmwood Ave.
881-6819
$$

Crowded into Kuni's narrow storefront premises are five tiny tables and a curved sushi bar with ten stools. Japanese wine bottles, boxes, sushi boards and dishes fill the shelves behind the bar and tiny saki cups each different, are pigeonholed into squares, looking more decorative that utilitarian. Sushi can be ordered in designated combinations of pieces and rolls, or individually. Pieces are short cylinders of pressed rice topped with slices of a wide variety of fish such as tuna, yellow tail, salmon, squid, or grilled eel, or by avocado, salmon roe, tofu, radish sprouts or tamago (egg), to name a few. Rolls are long cylinders of pressed rice wrapped around wafer thin slices of fish or vegetables and sliced into pieces of four or six. Sushi is served on a wooden, footed sushi block in orderly rows, garnished with a dollop of hot green horseradish and slivers of ginger. Miso soup, a base of high protein soybean paste with fermented barley or rice, changes daily. Half a dozen salads, like the four sea vegetables on mesclun with miso or ginger dressing, are offered. Other dishes include tempura (deep fried vegetables and seafood with a soy dipping sauce), tofu stuffed dumplings, grilled skewered chicken, and a seafood stir fry with shrimp, scallops, crab and little neck clams in a ginger sauce.

Left Bank
511 Rhode Island St.
882-3509
$$

On the west side of Richmond Avenue, that separator of fashionable with less fashionable Buffalo, Left Bank celebrates rather than apologizes for its location by its name. In one of Buffalo's oldest sections, the chic storefront with its exposed interior brick walls hung with large, colorful canvases, is more reminiscent of a New York City neighborhood restaurant than almost any other Buffalo eatery. Understated elegance without snobbery and a refined ambiance describe this dining experience. Most of the entrees are specials and change daily. Some specials may include the pecan and dijon encrusted chicken with wild rice or the roasted rack of lamb with a white bean and wild mushroom ragout. The excellent menu includes grilled meats like the black Angus strip steak, which can be served with sauteed mushrooms and cabernet demiglaze or on grilled Tuscan bread with glazed red onions and fontina cheese. Some smaller plates are rosemary risotto with grilled smoked chicken; artichoke stuffed portobello mushrooms; and crab cakes. Pasta dishes include tagliatelle with tomatoes, mushrooms, garlic, white wine and chicken; and fusilli with julienned vegetables, lemon-black pepper cream and rock shrimp. Focaccia comes with colorful combinations of fresh, grilled or roasted vegetables and meats along with a variety of cheeses. Desserts are wonderfully sumptuous. A string quartet entertains at Sunday brunches. *(See also: Nightlife)*

Little Talia Trattoria
1458 Hertel Ave.
833-8667
$$

Little Talia's chic, intimate interior packs everything in like a great cocktail party at a two-room New York City apartment. The open kitchen, tiny bar, pianist and several booths are on the main floor with additional seating available on the balcony. The Zuppa e pane, a homemade soup and crusty bread, changes daily and may be a thick, rich black and red bean soup. All pasta dishes are family recipes from the Abruzzi district of Italy, such as the homemade pasta in a a carrot-based tomato sauce; the cannelloni filled with spinach, goat cheese, sundried tomato and asiago cream sauce; or the lasagna of six different vegetables layered with cheese and a tomato-basil sauce. Dinners include veal Marsala with portobellos served with a roasted garlic risotto pancake; chicken breast marinated in balsamic vinegar, sauteed with veal demiglaze and served on angel hair pasta with wilted field greens; and occasionally, homemade Abruzzi-style sausage with dandelion greens and asiago cheese simmered in a burgundy wine demiglaze. Several versions of pizza rustica are offered including a rustic baked focaccia with a base of romano and asiago cheeses and roasted garlic. Desserts include homemade sorbet with flavors like strawberry and tangerine served with thin, crisp Italian biscuits.

Mastman's Kosher Delicatessen and Restaurant
1322 Hertel Ave.
876-7570
$

Mastman's is Western New York's only kosher eating establishment and features sandwiches, soups and sides. The restaurant, furnished with chrome and formica dining sets, is open from morning to early evening. Selections of hearty corned beef, Romanian and shoulder pastrami, tongue, fresh chopped liver, beef brisket, and liverwurst are combined in a variety of over-stuffed sandwiches on genuine Jewish rye or a roll, and are served with all-you-can-eat crisp, mild kosher dill pickles and sauerkraut. Fish salad sandwiches include the pungent chopped herring salad, the sweeter whitefish salad, and tuna. Lox are served with cream cheese on rye. Sides of either creamy style or sweet and sour cole slaw, potato or macaroni salad make good sandwich accompaniments. Knishes, (baked rounds of dough stuffed with either potatoes or kasha) pair well with the homemade matzo ball soup, a chicken soup with sliced carrots and huge, three inch dumplings made with matzo meal and cooked in the soup. Other homemade soups include; beef cabbage, bean and beef lentil. Genuine halvah, the confection of crushed sesame seeds in a sweet honey base, is sold by the pound, cut from a huge cream and tan block.

May Jen Chinese Restaurants
810 Elmwood Ave.
881-0038
$

Reached by an outside enclosed brick stairway, May Jen's dining rooms are on the second and third floors of a tastefully transformed Elmwood Avenue residence. The light and airy interior combines views of the treetops through vast expanses of glass and features original

also:
47 Kenmore Ave.
Amherst
832-5162

architectural details such as the chestnut staircase and fireplaces. An atmosphere of serenity and peace prevails. May Jen's broad menu goes beyond the usual. Unique soups include the velvet chicken corn and subgum winter melon. Six dumpling selections are offered including dim sum, vegetables and pork in pasta with oyster sauce, three varieties of barbecued spare ribs and cold sesame noodles. The house specialties include shrimp and scallops with pineapple and peppers; pressed duck stuffed and served with oyster sauce; and the showy Nesting in Paradise, a deep fried nest of potato strips filled with bright red lobster, shrimp, scallops, and vegetables served with a choice of four sauces. Other popular dishes include the Chicken Amazing with greens and black bean sauce; and spicy tangerine chicken, a *Taste of Buffalo* specialty. Meatless selections are of sufficient number to satisfy the vegetarian palate.

The Metropolitan
716 Elmwood Ave.
882-0772
$$

Set back from the street in the old post office building, The Metropolitan is a bit hard to see from the street. The deep patio area in front provides a great, mid-Elmwood summer gathering place. The checkered floor, black rimmed bar, ample black "leather" booths and chairs, crisp white linen and murals of famous metropolitan skylines in silhouette, are all part of the black and white decor. Cuisine focuses principally on sophisticated pasta dishes, with secondary emphasis on gourmet pizza and imaginative entrees. The whole roasted garlic bulb with brie and fresh foccacia; and the flash fried calimari strips with chipotle-lime mayonnaise are representative appetizers. One of the gourmet pizzas is the caramelized onion, mushroom, roasted red pepper and gorgonzola cheese over a sundried tomato-pesto base. Pasta dishes might include homemade spinach ravioli filled with herb-ricotta cheese with a basil-pesto cream sauce and fresh vegetables; or the shrimp scampi over capellini. Two of the rich, creative entrees are the pork tenderloin seared with leeks and pears in a creamy cider reduction with dried sweet cherry risotto; and the cashew crusted red snapper with sauteed spinach and beurre blanc sauce. A vegetarian specialty is offered daily.

Ming Teh
126 Niagara Blvd.
Fort Erie
Ontario, Canada
$ (with exchange)

Ming Teh is just over the Peace Bridge and about two blocks up Niagara Boulevard toward the Falls. The one-story building is decorated with brightly colored Chinese tiles and the interior is hung with paintings by owner/artist Sui Kui Cheung. Many consider Ming Teh the finest Chinese restaurant in the area. The creative menu features several soups including saki wine soup with shrimp, pork, vegetables and red dates. Ming Teh's exemplary Happy Family, on the menu for over twenty years, is a combination of shrimp, chicken and beef with Chinese vegetables, in a savory garlic and bean paste sauce served in an earthen pot. The stir-fried chicken with bean paste, cashews and almonds is a classic Northern Chinese sweet dish. Beef with tangerine peel and garlic is fierce and highly-spiced with chili pepper. Sweet and sour sauteed pork is prepared properly at Ming Teh and is nothing like the common battered version served elsewhere. Szechuan-style kang-po shrimp is a hot, sweet and sour blend of fried shrimp, water chestnuts, bamboo shoots, and dry lily flowers. Vegetarian dishes include pa pao chai, made with dried bean curd. Reservations are recommended.

Niagara Café

525 Niagara St.
885-2233
$

One of the few Hispanic restaurants in Buffalo, the Niagara Café serves primarily Puerto Rican cuisine. The restaurant is clean and bright, with large windows and shiny white tiles along the dining counter. With the spicy sounds of Latin rhythms playing in the background, diners may choose from a number of interesting appetizers. Pasteles, a tasty meat and banana pie, is a spongy dough sock filled with meat, potatoes and peas in a savory sauce. Other starters include octopus salad and stuffed potato. Specialties of the house include a dinner of boiled green bananas or fried plantains with roasted pork; or fried shrimp with crispy plantain chips. Other specials rotate daily with a variety of stews dominating. Weekends feature Salcocho, a stew of pigs feet, plantains and potatoes; and Cabrito en Fricase, goat stew. All of the Hispanic dishes at the Niagara are infused with the care that comes with home-cooked meals.   frb

Old Orchard Inn

2095 Blakeley
Corners Rd.
East Aurora
652-4664
$$$

The Old Orchard Inn is a low, brown-shingled, circa 1901 former hunting lodge set on 25 acres south of the Village of East Aurora. Converted into a tea room in 1931 and a full restaurant in the 1950's, for generations it has been the epitome of the genteel, country dining experience. Original fieldstone fireplaces warm the two dining rooms and chintz-curtained casement windows overlook the rolling, meadow-like grounds and pond. A lovely flagstone terrace adjoins the barroom. Inn traditions include a generous basket of warm, homemade cinnamon and dinner rolls; an immense platter of cheeses, fresh fruits, vegetables and dips; and the perfect Caesar salad. With the notable exception of one or two pasta dishes added in the last few years, most of the menu's character has remained; and menu items like the chicken fricassee with biscuits, chicken pot pie, rack of lamb and the sumptuous prime rib of beef have not changed in decades. Vegetables, such as the famous Harvard beets are served family-style. The heavenly lemon angel pie has been an Old Orchard favorite since 1931. Service is particularly gracious.

Old Red Mill
8326 Main St.
Clarence
633-7878
$$

The Old Red Mill, known for its abundance of decorative antiques, is named after the full scale water wheel that revolves under a spotlight in the front yard of this circa 1868 house. An authentic red caboose flanks one side of the building and a yellow passenger car the other. The interior's low-ceilinged rooms, wide floor- boards and fireplaces are reminiscent of a quaint New England inn. The menu concentrates on familiar meats and seafood. Prawns, clams casino, onion soup and an excellent seafood bisque are some starters. Poultry includes several chicken dishes, roasted duckling and turkey. Red meats include prime ribs au jus, steaks, like the Montreal del Monico, and seafood stuffed sirloin. Veal Anna, a house specialty, combines veal with lobster, mushrooms and artichoke hearts in a sherry-cream sauce. The Red Mill serves uncomplicated seafood plates like poached salmon, and snow crab clusters as well as more creative dishes like scallops with tomatoes, olives, scallions and mushrooms over spinach fettucini; and seafood Newburg over puff pastry. All-you-can-eat crab is served on Wednesdays and Fridays and several entrees have lower prices on Sundays. Authentic French desserts are from Croquembouche, a fine pastry shop in Clarence.

Oliver's Restaurant
2095 Delaware Ave.
877-9662
$$$$

A Buffalo landmark since 1936, Oliver's was established decades ago as the place where the chic Buffalo elite gather to see and be seen. Renowned for its fine cuisine, Oliver's simulates the decor and ambiance of a sophisticated New York restaurant. In an atmosphere soft with greys, blacks and mirrors, the cushioned circular bar dominates the front room where sleek suited men and women, invariably dressed in black, await their tables to the tune of the pianist at the baby grand. Dining in the barroom is in semi-circular booths of faux black leather or at tables crowded intimately into the back dining room. Service is brisk, friendly and professional and includes an immediate tiny hors d'oeuvre followed by a basket of excellent breads. Representative appetizers are: grilled sea scallops with arugula; the superb smoked pheasant spring roll on baby greens; a napoleon of wild mushrooms with truffle vinaigrette; and, extravagantly, a service of Osetra caviar. Soups may include tomato with an open-faced spinach and ricotta ravioli. Entrees include grilled breast of duckling with maple sweet potatoes and a tart cherry sauce; tournedos of beef tenderloin with truffled twice-baked potatoes and shallot glaze; or lobster with dill-lemon sauce, and goat cheese ravioli. The baked Alaska with chocolate and caramel sauces is a house specialty. Oliver's fine wine cellar is highly regarded.

Osaka Sushi Bar and Grille
3112 Main St.
831-0443
$$

Osaka is located near the SUNY Buffalo campus on the strip of Main Street that is becoming a lesser version of Elmwood Avenue. The side entrance through the gate is flanked by a traditional Japanese garden. Amidst the ivory walls and black woodwork are linen and glass covered tables and a sushi bar that seats nine, each place set precisely with a square black lacquered tray and chopsticks. At the bar, diners watch the two sushi chefs build the sculptured sushi creations. Servers have the loveliness of Japanese woodcut figures as they gracefully answer questions, make recommendations, and educate the unknowing. Sushi rolls can be ordered either in preselected combinations of six or ten, or individually from the 44 selections on the menu. Try saba (mackerel), tamago (egg), the avocado roll, the shrimp and asparagus roll or the soft-shell crab roll. Sushi is presented artistically on a footed wooden tray, garnished with slivers of rose-colored ginger and pale green hot Japanese horseradish. The khaki-fry, fried oysters in a crisp, light breading with tonkatsu sauce, is an excellent choice; and gyozo, traditional dumplings filled with vegetables and meat paste, is a good sized portion for the price. The miso soup is excellent. The Bento box is a meal in a compartmentalized black and vermillion lacquer box. The six sections of the box hold salmon, California rolls, peppered rice, breaded shrimp with yam, salad and pale green horseradish. Entrees include chicken teriyaki, calamari, steak and lobster, grilled eel, lobster or shrimp tempura. Osaka is casually elegant, serene and interesting with a wide range of prices and a menu that will satisfy the adventuresome as well as the cautious.

Oscar's Inn on the Lake
S4914 Lake Shore Rd.
Hamburg
627-5561
$$$

Looking something like an architecturally designed fisherman's shanty, Oscars clings to a stony cliff on Lake Erie. Every table has access to the unsurpassed lake view, and the sparkling waters, glowing sunsets and twinkling lights of Buffalo in the distance are the decor. The restaurant is expansive and rambling, with several dining rooms, a popular bar, and an outdoor patio. Oscar's menu ranges from formal dinners to sandwiches and snacks. Clams casino, shrimp cocktail, steamed and raw clams and raw oysters are some of the starters. Diners can create their own pasta dishes by selecting a choice of pasta sauces such as alfredo, marinara and pesto and additional ingredients like shrimp, chicken and artichoke hearts. Sandwiches range from burgers to trendy combinations. Lobster, shrimp and fish are some seafood dinner choices but chicken, chops and steaks are given equal billing. Prime rib is served on the weekends and a fish fry on Fridays. With a few exceptions, dinners are prepared in the traditional manner. The atmosphere is casual, sometimes noisy, and cheery.

Park Lane
33 Gates Cir.
881-2603
$$$

Dining at the landmark Park Lane, newly and brilliantly remodeled and under strong new ownership, is an aesthetic as well as social and culinary experience. The interior dining room, or Great Room, of the English Tudor style structure, has a cathedral ceiling and is dominated by an immense, copper-hooded fireplace. The sunken bar room, done in rich woods, earth red and copper with tiny, parchment-shaded lamps on the black bar is strikingly handsome. The Tavern, or front dining room, couples rich draperies with dark wood, and a soft deep couch sits before a blazing corner fireplace. A third dining room, the brick-walled Armory, was recently fitted as a wine room. The menu's extensive list of appetizers meld into its heartier entrees and are complimented by a long list of beers and wines by the glass, thus encouraging a leisurely, many-coursed approach to dining. Appetizers include eggplant, caviar and hummus with grilled breads; zucchini and radicchio pizza; and the duck confit with olive, citrus and avocado crostini. The Mediterranean fish soup in a tomato-saffron base is excellent. Lighter dishes include the potato gnocchi with tomato and mozzarella; rock shrimp and pea risotto; and penne with lamb and black olive ragout. Two of the fish entrees are the Atlantic seared cod with mashed potatoes; and the soy marinated grilled tuna with asparagus and fried leeks. Some robust entrees are the spiced pork chop with horseradish potatoes; roast leg of lamb with a carrot confit and boiled Yukon potato; and the balsamic marinated tenderloin with macaroni and spinach. An interesting array of sides includes roast squash and cauliflower, grilled asparagus; and sauteed spinach.

Peabody's
423 Elmwood Ave.
881-6228
$$$

Peabody's, a jewel of a restaurant, represents Buffalo's cosmopolitan good life. Its tiny dining area is expanded in the summer by a large outdoor covered deck in back, surrounded by handsome red brick structures and shaded by a giant black walnut tree. Food is exquisitely prepared with a light hand and the menu changes frequently. The gazpacho and the salad of Romaine, roasted red peppers, walnuts, and goat cheese are excellent. Crab cakes with remoulade sauce; snow crab claws with three sauces; and grilled mako shark marinated in Middle Eastern spices served with basmati rice, are some of the prize appetizers. Entrees include the tilapia fish sauteed with mango, ginger and rum with a macadamia nut sauce; the dramatic Portuguese style mussels cooked in a sauce of vegetables, prosciutto and chorizo sausage; and the crepes stuffed with ratatouille served with an herbed goat cheese cream sauce. Desserts like the B-52, a three-layer bombe of fudge-like cake, each layer incorporating a different liqueur; and a flourless chocolate cake with raspberry sauce, are well prepared in-house. Service at Peabody's is superior.

Pearl Street Grill and Brewery
76 Pearl St.
856-2337
$$

The Pearl Street Grill is situated in a handsomely restored red brick building below Church Street in the oldest area of downtown Buffalo. A micro-brewery, Pearl Street's copper-bellied, many tentacled kettle is visible though windows from inside and outside the restaurant. The broad, tin-ceilinged main bar/dining room has the air of a public room from the 1900's and is a popular meeting place for the downtown after work crowd and fans attending nearby sporting events at North Americare Park, and Marine Midland Arena. Not resting solely upon its success as a pub, Pearl Street's menu rivals that of any good restaurant. Dinner entrees, such as beer braised pot roast; charbroiled bratwurst and veal bockwurst served with mustard spaetzle and sauerkraut; and shepherd's pie with braised lamb, are all designed to accompany the beers made on premises. Gourmet pizzas and hearty sandwiches are also served. On many Friday nights, music is performed by local musicians.
(See also: Nightlife)

Polish Villa II
1085 Harlem Rd.
822-4908
Cheektowaga
$$
also:
2954 Union Rd.
Cheektowaga
683-9460

Polish Villa II is located in a half-timbered, turreted building with leaded glass windows, and an elaborate mirrored oak bar that was hand-carved in Poland. Mannequins display Polish national dress and a large painting depicts Polish scenes and customs. The atmosphere is warm and plush. On weekends, patrons dance on the small central dance floor to live music from the brass-railed gallery. Polish starters include the duck blood soup, a sweet, dark, rich and savory soup with thick kluski noodles. Platters combine golabki (stuffed cabbage); kielbasa sausage, potato pancakes and pierogi, filled with meat, cheese or vegetables. The piersi kurze w sosie winnym is a chicken breast stuffed with sausage dressing topped with mushroom sauce. Broiled scrod is offered Polish style and sliced tenderloin and beef kabob are served over kluski noodles. Non-Polish fare like roast Long Island duckling, lobster tail, stuffed sole and filet mignon are available and prime rib is prominently featured.

Protocol
6766 Transit Rd.
Williamsville
632-9556
$$

A stucco and green-awninged modern restaurant and banquet facility on busy Transit Road, Protocol is a friendly place that specializes in fresh seafood flown in daily from Boston. Dominating the appetizers are seafood selections like oysters Rockefeller, lemon pepper-crusted scallops, and coconut jumbo shrimp with raspberry sauce. From the grill come steaks, pork and lamb chops, chicken and barbecued ribs, as well as filet mignon stuffed with rock shrimp and served with mornay sauce. The pasta and seafood selections are expansive. Fettucine Alfredo can be served with blackened chicken, shrimp or sea scallops. Yellowfin tuna and Atlantic salmon are featured. Specialty dishes include scallops with spinach, fresh tomatoes and herb cream sauce over pasta. Light fare includes steak and chicken sandwiches, beef on weck, burgers, wings and an excellent classic Caesar salad. Desserts are created daily; the fruit cobblers are one excellent choice.

Ristorante Lombardo
1198 Hertel Ave.
873-4291
$$$

On Hertel Avenue for over 25 years, Lombardo's has evolved from a neighborhood bar into a fine dining establishment. The recent expansion added a handsome front room with curved French doors and an elevated patio for outdoor dining. The warm and welcoming atmosphere is genuine, much of the staff having been at Lombardo's for decades. Many classic favorites are represented on the menu, with some unique interpretations. Oysters Rockefeller are laced with anisette. Escargot in garlic, sherry and brandy sauce are served in sauteed mushroom caps. The sausage and fennel soup, not always offered, is delicious. One outstanding entree, the Continental, is half portions of veal Francese and scampi served together. Other entrees include Veal Marsala, layered with prosciutto and mozzarella; and sliced beef tenderloin with a mustard and a rosemary crust. Pasta and rice dishes include farfalle with salmon and peas in a vodka sauce and a risotto dish that changes daily. Cioppino, mixed seafood in a saffron fish broth is served with garlic croutons and risotto. Desserts include tiramisu; biscotti with fresh fruit; and the house specialty, frou frou cake, a white genoise cake layered with white chocolate mousse and topped with chocolate shavings.

Romanello's Roseland
490 Rhode Island St.
882-3328
$$

Romanello's Roseland has been a west side landmark for over sixty years, since 1963 in its present incarnation. The exterior is brilliant with floodlights and a canopy covers the carpet from curb to door. The doorman welcomes patrons crossing from the lighted parking lot. The former residence is a series of dining rooms on two levels, some expansive, some intimate, and the atmosphere is warm and casually formal. Start with one of the excellent soups, the minestrone that's always available; or a soup du jour like the spinach gorgonzola. The fresh baked bread with butter and herbed oil is a tasty accompaniment. The menu consists primarily of Italian gourmet pasta dishes. Entrees are served as light plates or as full dinners, the former is a smaller, yet still generous portion at a lower price. The vegetable lasagna with spinach is rolled rather than layered and the Manicotti Joseph varies the familiar dish by topping it with rock shrimp. Other familiar dishes are shrimp fra diavolo and tortellini primavera. Meat and seafood entrees include veal Angelo sauteed with cognac; broiled rack of lamb; and a seafood platter of white fish, shrimp scampi, broiled scallops and clams casino. Romanello's features a dinner for two at a reduced price. For dessert, the tiramisu is delicious.

The Roycroft Inn
40 South Grove St.
East Aurora
652-5552
$$$

In the center of the Village of East Aurora, surrounded by the handsome stone Roycroft Campus buildings, is The Roycroft Inn. The Inn was "open to friends" in 1905 to accommodate the thousands who flocked to East Aurora to participate in writer and philosopher Elbert Hubbard's Roycroft Arts and Crafts movement, which he founded in 1895 *(see: Day Trips).* After his dramatic death on the sinking Lusitania in 1915, the Inn went through several meta-morphoses and more than once it, too, was on the brink of disaster. In 1986, the Inn was granted National Landmark Status and was reopened in 1995 as a restaurant and inn, having been rescued and faithfully restored by charitable foundations. In warm weather, meals are served on the peristyle, the columned, open porch overlooking a garden courtyard on one side and South Grove Street on the other. Authentic Arts and Crafts style furniture graces the lobbies, the dining rooms and the sumptuously appointed guest rooms, which are booked well in advance. Dominating the south lobby are the beautiful, faithfully restored murals by Roycroft painter Alexis Fournier. the Larkin Room, the windowed corridor that overlooks the courtyard, links the north and south lobbies and is wide enough for a dozen tables. The handsome rear dining room is made cozy in the winter by the original stone fireplace. The eclectic American menu is dominated by meat, although chicken, fish and vegetarian entrees are also represented. The Inn offers almond encrusted rack of lamb with rosemary glaze, and a surf and turf of grilled tenderloin tips and red crab claws tossed with garlic, tomatoes, leeks, asparagus and pasta. Grilled rainbow trout with lime pecan butter are accompanied by sweet potato chips, while sauteed medallions of veal are joined with shrimp provencale.

Rue Franklin
341 Franklin St.
852-4416
$$$

The famous French genius for style is unmistakable at this genuinely French restaurant just steps from the theatre district. Decor is charmingly sophisticated. Bistro chairs and tables on creaking floors surround the tiny, central, half-moon bar. A larger, softer dining room is at the front. A handful of tables overlook the enchanting walled garden and the summer dining patio out back. True French liberality is represented by an atmosphere of elegance without snobbery. Dede and Joe Lippes change the menu seasonally and everything on it is appealing. Each entree is carefully and imaginatively conceived and brilliantly prepared. Appetizers might include the celery root and crabmeat salad; or a timbale of pasta, shiitake mushrooms and ricotta with a mushroom cream sauce. Entrees may include monkfish with roasted beets and bok choy; veal tenderloin medallions with pineapple and curry; venison with pepper sauce; or the understated filet mignon with shallots and a potato pancake. Desserts like mascarpone crepes served with port sauce and apple tarte with caramel ice cream, are outstanding. Excellent service is in the old-school manner.

Salvatore's Italian Gardens
6461 Transit Rd.
Depew
683-7990
$$$

In what may be the supreme example of style over substance, Salvatore's Italian Gardens has become one of the most renowned restaurants in upstate New York. From the moment one passes through the revolving doors into the grand foyer, there is a realization that subtlety was not a word found in the interior designer's vocabulary. The room is dominated by an absolutely massive chandelier that seems to extend to the floor, a precursor to the chandelier theme that runs throughout the restaurant. Once past the foyer, the size of Salvatore's begins to become evident. The dining rooms, that seat nearly 400 for dinner, and the three large banquet rooms are filled with columns, ruffled curtains and the ever present chandeliers. Although the restaurant's motto is "we love to overdo it," and they have a reputation for being over-the-top, the look is actually much more subdued and elegant than the old restaurant that was damaged by fire in 1994. Much of the statuary is gone as is the famous three-dimensional panorama of moonlit Rome. Nevertheless, only at Salvatore's will you find a hallway with Remington bronze replicas depicting scenes of the American West, across from a print from Michelangelo's Sistine Chapel, which is alongside church confessionals that have been converted into phone booths. With this overwhelming decor, it's only natural that the food would take a back seat. The menu, presented by the tuxedo-clad wait staff, includes classic Italian veal dishes like ossobuco, saltimbocca, and parmigiana; chicken entrees like: Marsala, Rollitini (with spinach and ham) and Neptune (stuffed with seafood topped with a lobster dill sauce); and pasta dishes. In addition there are steaks, chops and numerous seafood selections. The dishes are adequately prepared and nicely presented. Under the meticulous eye of owner Russ Salvatore, the strong points here are expert service, cleanliness and an attention to detail, not expected at a restaurant of this size.

frb

San Marco Restaurant
2082 Kensington Ave.
Snyder
839-5876
$$$

San Marco, a quiet, conservatively styled restaurant in a pleasant residential neighborhood, seamlessly balances cuisine, atmosphere and service. The well-mannered ambiance is elegant rather than snobbish. Its unparalleled cuisine is highly creative and flawlessly prepared, and the long list of daily specials is supported by a menu of successful favorites. The fragrant quaglia in padella, (quail, sauteed in cognac and shallots then grilled), is served as an appetizer with porcini mushroom and truffle sauce or as an entree over wild mushroom risotto. The antipasta mista combines prosciutto from Parma, sopressata salami, fresh buffalo mozzarella, olives and artichokes. First courses may include spinach and cheese ravioli with tiger shrimp sauteed in cognac with a creamy sun dried tomato sauce; or spinach tagliatelle with salmon in a light cream sauce. Frequently available are the tenderloins of wild boar marinated in olive oil, garlic and juniper berries, and fresh de-boned wild rabbit prepared with a wild mushroom sauce. More docile entrees include saltimbocca alla romana, veal sauteed in white wine and sage and topped with a veil of mozzarella and prosciutto; and fresh fillet of sole in a creamy tomato sauce with capers and wine. The caramelized pear tart with vanilla ice cream fits the standard of excellent understated desserts.

Schwabl's
789 Center Rd.
West Seneca
674-9821
$

Schwabl's has looked the same for years, and probably hasn't changed much since 1942 when Ray Schwabl moved the restaurant to West Seneca from Buffalo's old German section. The Schwabls have been restauranteurs in the Buffalo area since 1837, and may be the longest line of restaurant operators in New York State. The front of the converted white clapboard house contains the bar, several tables and the steam table on which the huge steamboat roast of beef is carved into paper thin slices by carver Dave Brown. Owner Ray Schwabl Jr. presides over the bar and welcomes patrons, his thatch of silver hair a match for his spotless white butcher's apron. The 1940's decor is nostalgic and the dozen or so tables are always filled. The service is warm, friendly and efficient, and the attire is casual. The menu revolves around the excellent quality roast beef, offering beef on kummelweck, a hot roast beef sandwich with bread and gravy and a roast beef plate. The homemade hot German potato salad is exceptionally good as is the sweet and creamy homemade cole slaw. Yellow pike, haddock, fried scallops, french fried shrimp and combination seafood plates are also great favorites. On Saturday nights, Hungarian goulash with dumplings is served. Reservations are never taken, but the wait is pleasant, never too long, and always well rewarded. Schwabl's is a "don't miss" Buffalo restaurant, and a bargain to boot.

Sequoia
718 Elmwood Ave.
882-2219
$$$

Like a proud mother, Bob Mollot, chef and co-owner of Sequoia with his wife Sarah, likes to comment that the plates come back to his kitchen empty. Dinner at the Sequoia is like eating Mom's cooking--the idealized mom, that is, who studied at the Culinary Institute and worked under a famous chef in San Francisco. The result is California-inspired American home cooking. Sequoia's meatloaf is served with mashed red potatoes and wilted spinach, while the garlic and chipotle rubbed featherbone steak comes with dry jack and cheddar potatoes along with a jicama and pepper slaw. One delicious offering is the grilled balsamic glazed yellowfin tuna over a warm apple smoked bacon vinaigrette and herb salad. A selection of lighter entrees at about half the price include; baby lamb chops with minted chutney, grilled adobe flatbread with pulled chicken, and tequila and lime marinated shrimp tostada with avocado and tomato salsa. The interior of the late Victorian house cum restaurant has a muted, soft atmosphere. The front room is dominated by the painting "Phoenicians in the Forest" by local artist Craig Larotunda. The focus of the second room is a carefully preserved oak fireplace with tile surround. Service is attentive and the atmosphere is casually elegant. Outdoor seating is available in warm weather.

Siena
4516 Main St.
Amherst
839-3108
$$$

Siena derives its name from the Tuscan city renowned for its art and architecture and one of the Renaissance's most powerful city-states. Colorful banners of centuries-old Sienese families hang from the ceiling of this restaurant's handsomely designed interior, and the main dining room is dominated by a monumental oil painting depicting the annual Sienese horse race that's run right through the city's piazza. Siena's atmosphere is both refined and relaxed. The menu is presented in the Italian manner, allowing the diner to choose a light meal of thin-crusted gourmet pizza for under $10, or indulge in a many-coursed dinner of antipasti, insalade, pasta, second courses and dessert. Pizza options include the Gamberi, a combination of rock shrimp, tomato and mixed cheeses or the Nicola, topped with eggplant caponata, goat cheese and fresh basil. Baked hot banana peppers stuffed with ricotta, anchovy, romano and gorgonzola is one of the appealing antipasti. Two creative pasta dishes are the linguine with dandelion greens, charred tomato and ricotta; and the Penne Romano, with chicken, oven dried tomatoes, prosciutto and sweet peas in a romano cream. Dinner entrees are prepared in the most sophisticated manner with delicate sauces, unusual cheeses and ingredients used in surprising but delicious combinations. Examples are the marinated, sauteed boneless chicken breast layered with roasted eggplant, montrachet, marinated tomato, spinach and sherry demi-glace, and the veal tenderloin with a sesame chive garlic crust and port wine sauce. Plate presentation is beautiful. Traditional Italian desserts such as tiramisu are made on premises.

Tandoori
7740 Transit
632-1112
$$

One of only a few Indian restaurants in the area, Tandoori is named after the tandoor oven in which many of its specialty items are prepared. Expansive and comfortable, the restaurant's interior is decorated with colorful textile wall hangings, weavings, and brightly painted wooden carvings. The menu has scores of choices from the appetizers, soups, and entrees. There are the usual basmati rice dishes, curries, breads, and kabobs cooked in the tandoor. Chicken, lamb and seafood are prepared in countless combinations with vegetables, nuts and herbs and spices that may be unfamiliar to the Western palate. Many dishes are spicy and can be ordered hot, medium or mild. Tandoori has a special selection of dishes from some of India's 26 states, each with a uniquely different cuisine. Desserts include a classic milky rice pudding and an unusual spiced ice cream.

Village Pub
3974 Main St.
Strykersville
457-9545
$$

The Village Pub occupies Strykersville's old hotel and is one of the handful of businesses in the tiny Wyoming County farming community just minutes from East Aurora. One hundred years ago, the hotel was the main stopping place for cattle drovers who marched their cattle up the center of the road from the Southern Tier to Buffalo's East Side stockyards. Today, the Strykersville cattle corrals are gone and the livery is now the Pub's parking lot. The Pub's wood-paneled interior is hung with antique farming paraphernalia and retains the flavor and hospitality of the old hotel dining room, well worth a trip to the country. The menu is right in step and ranges from a full array of steaks and prime rib to seafood, including the Friday night fish fry. There's also chicken, several good Italian dishes, subs and pizzas. They serve excellent homemade soups, hot and cold sandwiches, burgers and a long list of appetizers including battered mushrooms with horseradish sauce and mini tacos. The soup and salad bar is well stocked and features crusty homemade breads and sweet varieties like lemon, banana nut and pumpkin breads. Desserts include the excellent homemade fruit and ice cream pies. Pastries, coffee cakes, pies and breads are also sold in the adjoining bakery and gift shop.

Water Valley Inn
S6656 Gowanda St. Rd.
Hamburg
649-9691
$$

Just outside the Village of Hamburg in the hamlet of Water Valley, the Water Valley Inn has been a functioning inn for 122 years, although it no longer hosts overnight guests. Formerly the site of a stagecoach stop next to Eighteen Mile Creek, Water Valley has retained some rustic remnants of its historical past. The inn's atmosphere is comfortable and neighborly. The fare begins with appetizers and snacks like smoked salmon with dill sauce, battered cauliflower or zucchini "circles," and moves on to hot and grilled sandwiches, salads and stir fries, and ends with full dinner entrees like steaks, chops and seafood. Dinner choices include a generous, economical prime rib dinner, ham steak, liver and onions and marinated chicken breast served five ways. Pies, different each day, are genuinely homemade.

West End Inn
340 Union St.
Hamburg
649-2446
$$

The West End Inn is an authentically restored 130-year old "drummers" or traveling salesman's hotel near the railroad tracks in the Village of Hamburg. Its history and style is its principal charm and the large, horseshoe bar draws a large suburban crowd on the weekends. The handsome dining room has a copper stamped ceiling, bare floors and the original tables and chairs. Overflow crowds eat in one of the large banquet rooms. Food ranges from pasta, seafood, red and white meats, to an extensive hearty sandwich and salad menu. Weekend specials, seem to be a draw for the local regulars.

Woo Chon Korean Restaurant
402 Evans Street
Evenstown Plaza
Williamsville
626-5980
$$

As of this writing, Woo Chon is the only full service Korean restaurant in the Buffalo area. Much Korean food is first marinated then grilled or sauteed, differing from that of neighboring China and Japan. The Korean diet is dominated by large quantities of vegetables, fin and shell fish and of course, rice. Woo Chon's bright and modern interior has three booths with hooded barbecue grills at the center of the table at which patrons grill for themselves dishes like marinated prime ribs, chicken, pork or tongue. Served along with the marinated meats are rice, saucers of soy dip, a pot of clear bean sprout soup, a basket of leaf lettuce, and seven saucers of Korean vegetables, different every day. Some of vegetable selections may include marinated sliced cabbage and radish, large and small bean sprouts, cucumber, shredded potato and carrot, and seaweed. Diners roll any combination of the food spread before them into a lettuce leaf and dip the roll in the soy dip. Soups that make a meal are the whe dup bap, sliced raw fish, vegetables and rice with vinegar hot sauce; and samgae-tang, broiled chicken with chestnut, dried Chinese dates and garlic. Noodles are very thin and served cold with combinations of vegetables, fish, beef and hot sauce. Fish entrees include broiled yellow croaker, king fish, mackerel, salmon and cod. Monk fish is simmered with bean sprouts in a spicy garlic sauce. Some dishes are for the adventurous, such as the raw skate-wing fish in hot spicy sauce, steamed pigs' feet in sauce, or barbecued cow's stomach. Barley tea is the beverage of choice.

X-Cel Produce
224 Elmwood Ave.
883-9235
$

X-Cel is a deli with equal proportions of attitude, intellect and good food. A narrow storefront at the gateway to Elmwood Avenue just north of North Street, X-Cel features 35 huge sandwiches on a variety of breads made with high quality ingredients and wrapped in white deli paper. The take-out menu is devoted to food, commentary and interesting trivia. Homemade soups change daily and 18 healthy salads such as veggie tortelli, wild rice, chicken mango and black bean are sold by the pound. Much of the business is take-out, but seating is available for about a dozen of X-Cel's many loyal patrons. One of Buffalo's few examples of an old-fashioned greengrocer, X-Cel sells hard-to-find produce, such as fresh herbs, mangos, French beans and ginger, as well as a good selection of high quality, more familiar produce. Family run since 1982, X-Cel receives little criticism, but, as the master of the last laugh, the menu lists a complaint number that turns out to be the community mental health services message.

Zuzon
5110 Main St.
Williamsville
634-6123
$$

Zuzon's is located in the Walker Center, an upscale strip mall just off the Thruway on Main Street. The name Zuzon evolved from "Zuzu's petals," from the film *It's a Wonderful Life*. Patrons and friends, believing that it has a zoo connection, made gifts of large and small animal statuary, which have become part of the beautifully designed interior. The creative menu is American eclectic with many ethnic groups called upon, including Italian, French, English, Mexican, Asian and Polish, with others standing in the wings to appear as the menu changes. Food to assuage all degrees of hunger is offered, from snacks and burgers to full course dinners, and patrons can sit at the grill for Zuzon's Z-burger or at a linen draped table for rotisserie herb chicken and rosemary roasted potatoes. Appetizers range from mussels de Provence to quesadillas. Pizzas can be topped with smoked salmon, red onion, tomato and capers. The entrees include such down-home favorites as meatloaf with peas and carrots, but with the added surprise of a cabernet sauce. Strip steak is served au poivre with ratatouille, pomme frite and hazelnut brandy sauce. Both Northern Italian and Sicilian pasta entrees are staples on the changing menu. Of course, beef, chicken and fish are always available from the grill. Zuzon's pervading sense of fun is evident in its playful presentation, which reflects a kind of child-like artistic creativity. Every meal should end with Zuzon's incomparably delicious desserts, which are made in house.

Cafés

CAFÉS

Bella Bean Cafe
3971 Main St.
Amherst
833-2326

Bella Bean, across the street from St. Benedict's Church in Amherst, is a pretty cafe, serving quality homemade meals and desserts. Amid the cool green color scheme are cafe tables with metal and wicker chairs where patrons may enjoy some unique coffee drinks like the snickers or banana split lattes. Much of the cafe's popularity is due to the lunches which include excellent soups, salads like the blackened chicken Caesar and specialty sandwiches. Desserts include homemade tarts, pastries, cakes and pies. In addition, the cafe serves homemade ice cream and chocolates.   frb

Cafe Aroma
957 Elmwood Ave.
884-4522
also: 5229 Main St.
Williamsville
631-2687

Cafe Aroma, a charming cafe with a warm and personal atmosphere, is a meeting place for creative Elmwood Avenue types, students and well-dressed city dwellers alike. One of Cafe Aroma's most attractive aspects is its inclusive rather than exclusive attitude. Its near perfect location on the corner of Elmwood and Bidwell Parkway affords views from windows and outdoor tables of the parkway's beautiful greenery. The many espresso and coffee drinks are well prepared and the coffees, cocoa, and flavored Italian syrups are of high quality. Masterful homemade cakes, tarts and tortes change daily and are temptingly displayed in glass cases. Tiramisu, made from homemade savoiardi (ladyfingers) soaked in espresso and layered in mascarpone, chocolate ganache and whipped cream is a house specialty. Full lunches and suppers of excellent homemade soups, pasta salads, sandwich wraps and panini are relished by Cafe Aroma's interesting city clientele.

Carriage Trade Pastries
1089 Elmwood Ave.
881-2326

A hidden treasure, Carriage Trade's diminutive shop is the source of many of the splendid desserts served in a number of Buffalo's best restaurants. All pastries are made with the finest natural ingredients. Sold by the slice or whole for important occasions, are the specialty cakes and tarts such as the mocha meringue torte, layers of nut meringue, coffee buttercream, chocolate and whipped cream or the lime blueberry tart, a walnut crust filled with lime custard and covered with blueberries. Some of the Carriage Trade's other offerings are cheesecakes, lemon squares, muffins, scones, cookies and breads. Lunch offerings consist of homemade soups combined with breads and scones, an example being the potato leek soup with a ginger-raisin scone. Coffee is limited to regular and decaf.

Coffee Bean Cafe
3268 Main St.
837-2326

The Coffee Bean Cafe has the feel of a college coffeehouse, as well it should, being just a stone's throw from UB. The narrow space is punctuated by the original artwork that adorns the walls. At the counter, several unique coffee drinks are offered including the oxymoronic frozen hot chocolate and the crow bar, which includes four shots of espresso, a obvious choice for pulling the all-nighter. The menu includes soups, salads, panini and changing specials. Tuesday through Saturday evenings, there's live music.   frb

The Java Temple
57 Allen St.
882-1250

In contrast to the ever proliferating upscale cafes, the dowdy atmosphere of Java Temple can be refreshing to those seeking a bohemian coffeehouse. At the counter there are the usual coffee concoctions, Italian sodas, cookies, cakes and pies along with a light menu that changes daily. Customers can enjoy meals and beverages while relaxing on the well-worn furniture, playing a board game or gazing out onto the always interesting corner of Allen and Franklin.

frb

Le Metro

520 Elmwood Ave.
885-1500
also:
5110 Main St.
Williamsville
631-2725
61 S. Buffalo St.
Hamburg
646-1636

Le Metro was named after the Paris subway system simply because it sounded good. Located on one of the Elmwood Strip's best corners, its handsome decor is dominated by a significant mythological painting. Le Metro has the comfortable atmosphere of a European neighborhood cafe. It specializes in creative sandwiches on marvelous breads, such as the turkey and sage cheddar with cranberry mayo; or the hummus, marinated tomato, cucumber and sprouts which can be on Roman chibatta or focaccia bread. The two soups du jour are always unusual and of highest quality. One example is the excellent cream of artichoke with chicken. The full range of coffees, lattes, espresso and cappuccino are served with lavish desserts, such as the chocolate truffle torte drizzled with chocolate, or the raspberry walnut torte. Le Metro's wonderful breads can be purchased bakery style.

Solid Grounds

431 Elmwood Ave.
882-5282

Solid Grounds is a bustling cafe on the corner of Elmwood Avenue and Bryant Street. Started by an ex-banker who would "rather grind beans than count them," the cafe is more than just coffee. Under the painted ceiling tiles in the bright cafe, or at the sidewalk tables in the summer, diners can choose from an interesting menu of well prepared dishes. Breakfast offerings include omelettes, French toast and whole wheat pancakes. Lunch features sandwiches served on homemade bread, quiche, salads and fresh soups. There's also an extensive vegetarian menu. The dinner menu changes seasonally, and far exceeds the basic coffeehouse fare. Some recent dishes included crab cakes with fresh tomato cilantro salsa, almond crusted chicken breast with mashed sweet potatoes and poached salmon in a honey mustard and dill sauce. frb

Spot Coffee
227 Delaware Ave.
854-7768

In a location between downtown and Allentown, Spot Coffee's unique decor includes an oversized mural of the cafe, blue and white checked tablecloths, windows hung with odd bits of fabrics and lined with 1950's coffee cups and a parlor furnished with overstuffed second-hand furniture. It promotes Seattle-style coffee and has a full and imaginative array of espresso, cappuccinos and lattes which it serves in large crockery cups and saucers. Homemade soup changes daily and a good selection of fruit, green, pasta, legume, grain and chicken salads are available. Sandwiches can be roll-ups, on bagels or focaccia bread. Gourmet pizzas such as the asparagus with four cheeses are also served. Coffee beans and paraphernalia are available. All of Buffalo's alternative press is represented.

Starbucks
933 Elmwood Ave.
882-5440
also: several other locations

No one can say that the coffee served at this or any of the other area Starbuck's that recently hit Buffalo isn't good. It is. But that's not the point. The new Starbuck's on Elmwood was the subject of hot controversy because of the fear that the wealthy out-of-state chain would steal business from locally owned establishments along the strip and send its profits out of town. It turns out that although carefully contrived, Starbuck's reconstituted coolness cannot hold a candle to the warmth, personal interest and excellent coffees, desserts and sandwiches of other Elmwood Avenue coffee houses. On one visit, even its live singer seemed apologetic. Desserts and cookies are locally made by Vito's and Starbuck's coffee can be purchased by the pound.

Stimulance
3160 Main St.
834-8207

"Stimulance," is not only an invented word, but an interesting coffeehouse and general hang-out. It's proximity to UB may be one reason for its draw of a very young crowd. Along with the usual coffee drinks are bagels and some baked goods. The entertainment scene is big with varying musicians and open mike Mondays.

frb

Sweet Tooth
478 Elmwood Ave.
884-2520

As its name implies, Sweet Tooth's emphasis is on desserts, with coffee as the accompaniment. The shop divides its attention between dessert cakes, tortes, tarts, flans, bombes, cookies, cheesecakes, ice cream and fine chocolates. One example of the 44 dessert selections, not all available each day, is the Toffee Kahlua Madness Torte, a toffee crusted creation layered with intensely chocolate cake and pale chocolate mousse which was the winner of the 1997 *Taste of Buffalo Chairman's Choice Award.* Another example is the Macadamia Nut Flan, which combines chocolate butter cream, whipped cream, shaved dark chocolate and chopped macadamia nuts over a toffee and macadamia nut flan base. Familiar and not so familiar cheesecakes like the Black Forest, pistachio and linzer are also made here. Desserts can be purchased by the slice or whole. Espresso, cappuccino, mochaccino, cafe latte, and flavored lattes are served as well as plain and flavored cocoas. A good selection of fine chocolates are sold by the pound or in boxed assortments. Half of Sweet Tooth's shop is devoted to its rousing ice cream business, and crowds line up for cones, sundaes, shakes and other fancy concoctions, making it a happy neighborhood gathering place.

Tiger Lily & Wing
37 Allen St.
881-1164

This unique Asian bakery is situated on the first floor of the stately home that once belonged to Dr. Matthew Mann, the doctor called on to attend President McKinley when he was shot in 1901. In a small front room is the service counter, where fresh baked Chinese buns are prominently displayed. Steamed buns, like the ones found on dim sum menus are offered along with baked sweet and savory buns with a variety of fillings. Savory buns include beef with black bean, and curried chicken, while examples of the sweet variety are the red bean paste or the almond. In addition to the buns, Tiger Lily serves a changing entree and soup for lunch. The dishes are primarily Asian-influenced and may include Indonesian, Vietnamese, Chinese or Korean ingredients, often fused with western touches. There are also cookies and pastries. The unique dishes and quality of preparation has made Tiger Lilly and Wing a popular spot with many restaurant professionals. Patrons may dine in the beautiful dining room, then wander through the antique shop. The cafe is open only until 6pm.

frb

Nightlife

NIGHTLIFE

Buffalo is an interesting city for many reasons, not the least of which is its paradoxical club scene. A former steel town with deep working class roots, Buffalo is also a haven to independent artists and assorted bohemian types, all of whom add greatly to the rich tapestry of Buffalo's cultural life. It is exactly the blending of these two rather diverse groups of people that comprises the heart of the city's nightlife. Whatever you fancy, odds are you'll find a bit of it here. Great bands--from blues to punk, folk to r&b--populate the Queen City's many live music clubs. DJ's spin everything from top 40 to acid jazz, country to hip hop. Hip and elegant jazz can be heard a stone's throw from a disco, and micro breweries can be found nestled comfortably between sports bars and corner watering holes. Buffalo is a tough town, and its inhabitants are tough as well. It's a city of extremes; the winters are hard, the summers hot and the people love to party, whatever the season. We're famous for snow, wings and good rock and roll. Here's where to find all of the above.

To find out specifically who's playing where and when, pick up a copy of one of the free weekly publications: *Artvoice* or *Buffalo Beat.*

NIGHTLIFE BY CATEGORIES

BLUES
Blues Room
Lafayette Tp.Rm.

CHIPPEWA DISTRICT
Atomic
Barrel House
Calumet
Coliseum
Kingsnake
67 West

CIGAR FRIENDLY
Coliseum
Havana

COUNTRY
Al-E-Oops

DJ
Atomic
Buddies
Coliseum
Continental
Funhouse
Kingsnake
Old Pink
67 West

JAZZ
Anchor Bar
Bijou Grille
Calumet
Colored Mus. Cl.
Dakota Grill
Left Bank
Tralfalmadore

LIVE MUSIC
Barcade
Broadway Joe's
Cellar Bar
Central Park
Club KC
Continental
Elmwood Lounge
Kingsnake
Merlin's
Mr. Goodbar
Mohawk Place
Nietzsche's
Shannon Pub

MICRO BREWS
Buffalo Brew Pub
Mr. Goodbar
Pearl Street

NIGHTLIFE

Al-E-Oops
5389 Genesee St.
Lancaster
681-0200

Mostly country, with a little western thrown in for good measure. Al-E-Oops is a casual hang, a good spot to tip back a few Budweisers in a homey unpretentious atmosphere. Known for its hickory-smoked barbecue.

Alternative Brews
3488 Sheridan Dr.
446-0424

Probably the best beer selection in town, and a home away from home to beer connoisseurs. Everything from domestic to imported beer, exotic ales and micro-brews are available in a casual atmosphere. A panacea for the beer lover.

Anacone's Inn
3178 Bailey Ave.
836-8905

A loveable hang-out with a great jukebox and an emphasis on pool and dart competitions, Anacone's is known as a great partying spot for students of the State University at Buffalo's Main Street campus. Hoppin' on Thursday, Friday and Saturday nights.

Anchor Bar
1047 Main St.
886-8920

A Buffalo legend, with a country-wide reputation as the home and original birth-place of the Buffalo chicken wing. No trip to Buffalo would be complete without a stop at the Anchor Bar. Weekends you'll hear some of the hottest jazz the city has to offer and enjoy a relaxed, informal and hospitable setting. Highly recommended. *(See also: Restaurants)*

Atomic
49 West Chippewa
849-4957

Atomic is one of the hippest places in town. It sports a decidedly New York City loft/warehouse space atmosphere. DJ's spin the latest in house, dance, techno, drum & base, and occasionally industrial music. Dancing is encouraged, and the clientele range from the upwardly mobile to the eternally youthful. A great Friday night spot.

Barcade
1620 Niagara Falls Blvd.
832-1620

A strip-mall type place with a loud in-house PA, much pool playing and dart throwing, and a clientele centered around big-haired girls and guys with huge muscles. Features live music, mostly cover bands and harder rock stuff, and is known as a place to dance on ladies' nights, which are usually on Wednesdays. Also hosts a 19-and-over night on Sundays.

The Barrel House
85 West Chippewa St.
856-4645

A drinking bar, in the truest sense of the words. No frills, no flash, no gimmicks. Just a casual, friendly atmosphere and a wide selection of beer and liquor. A perfect spot if you find yourself in the mood for such things.

Bijou Grille
643 Main St.
847-1512

An elegant and classy spot that serves top-notch American cuisine in a posh setting. Located right in the heart of the Theatre district, the Bijou is also renowned as one of the best jazz rooms in the city. It's a great place for a date or just an evening of refined debauchery. Highly recommended.

Blues Room at the Lafayette Hotel
391 Washington St.
855-2587

Not to be confused with the Lafayette Tap Room, the Blues Room is located in the historical Lafayette Hotel, an architectural landmark in downtown Buffalo. Like the Tap room, it hosts Blues exclusively, in this case concentrating on local talent more than national. There's an excellent beer selection and a great view of the stage from the bar, certainly things to consider when you go out for a night of deep blues. Recommended spot for a first date.

Broadway Joe's
3051 Main St.
836-9555

This place gets by on its decadent charm. Proprietor Broadway Joe is a colorful character and is more than willing to bend your ear, if he can catch it above the din of the Grateful Dead-styled bands his club regularly books. Highly frequented by the college set, Joe's is a Buffalo landmark.

Buddies
31 Johnson Park
855-1313

The most renowned gay club in Buffalo, and usually the spot where revelers end their night with fevered dancing and flamboyant entertainment. People of all sexual persuasions are welcome and the atmosphere is jubilant and inviting.

Buffalo Brew Pub
6861 Main St.
632-0552

A micro-brewery with a warm and inviting country decor. Feel free to toss your peanut shells on the floor as you sample the widest variety of micro-brew in the area. Also serves lunch and dinner. A beer drinker's delight.

The Calumet Arts Cafe
56 West Chippewa
855-2220

A posh place that offers fine dining as well as a wide array of local, national and international jazz, blues, folk and world music. The Calumet is a Buffalo legend. In the summer, its patio is one of the hottest in town. Anything goes, but the majority of the clientele dresses fairly nicely. Everyone from McCoy Tyner to Diana Krall has graced the Calumet stage, and the elegantly adorned and widely spaced tables make for a highly enjoyable dining and viewing experience. Highly recommended.

The Cellar Bar

(See: Pearl Street Brewery)

Central Park Grill
2519 Main St.
836-9466

A neighborhood bar with a ton of rustic charm, CPG features live music most nights of the week and cold pitchers every night. The decor is sloppily endearing, and the two floors make watching a band or casually conversing over drinks equally easy. Nothing fancy--just good old fashioned fun.

Club KC
2072 Kensington Ave.
839-9181

A rock club where, on any given night, you'll hear both original and cover bands on a state-of-the-art sound system. The Club hosts an intermingling of urban and suburban folk. Casual attire.

Club Marcella
Theatre Place
622 Main St.
847-6850

Flamboyant and eccentric, Club Marcella has become one of Buffalo's most talked about nightclubs since opening a mere 5 years ago. Host to weekly drag shows, Marcella encourages vibrant behavior in its patrons, who range from the curious to the unabashedly diva-esque. A night you surely won't forget.

Coliseum Entertainment Complex
257 Franklin
853-3600

Three floors and nearly half a dozen different clubs within the Coliseum Complex make it Buffalo's premier dance club. Long a point of debate among the Buffalo nightlife cognoscenti, the Coliseum packs'em in every weekend much to the detriment, many believe, to the original music club scene. Still, if dancing in the midst of Buffalo's "beautiful people" sounds like your idea of fun, this is the place for you.

The Colored Musicians Club
145 Broadway
855-9383

An old-school jazz room with a warm and inviting atmosphere, The Colored Musicians Club is another Buffalo landmark. Modeled after the Harlem jazz clubs of the late 50's and 60's, the club hosts the best in Buffalo jazz talent every weekend.

Cole's
1104 Elmwood Ave.
886-1449

See: Restaurants

Colter Bay Grill
561 Delaware Ave.
882-1330

Colter Bay is a restaurant specializing in southwestern-styled food, but it's also a popular nightspot offering a broad selection of brews. Located at one of the busiest cross-streets in Buffalo, Colter Bay is a nice spot for a first date or a night out drinking with friends. Clientele ranges from the young and professional to the college crowd.

The Continental
212 Franklin St.
855-3938

The Continental is a central part of Buffalo's rock history. Unflinchingly dingy, this two floor dive was home to the Goo Goo Dolls in the 80's and early 90's, and spawned most of the city's now diminished punk, hardcore and indie rock scene. Floor one is where you'll find a wide variety of local and national acts; floor two houses the most outrageous dance floor in town. No matter how you slice it, The Continental comes up cool. Dress in black, or you'll stick out like a sore thumb.

Dakota Grill
4224 Maple Rd.
Amherst
834-6600

The ritzy Dakota Grill was once the home of crooner Michael Civisca. With its posh surroundings, and adult crowd, it's now home to some of the best jazz and lounge music in the city and surrounding environs. Have plenty of room on your credit card if you want to enjoy Dakota to its fullest. It's not cheap, but then again, no one ever said class came for free.

Elmwood Restaurant Lounge & Bar
522 Elmwood Ave.
882-5881

Located in the heart of the Elmwood business district, the Elmwood Lounge has come to be known as the home of the amazing Lance Diamond Revue. A good time is guaranteed on weekend evenings, when the Diamond man brings his Vegas-styled show to this casual, low-key room. A great place for a high spirited time.

Essex St. Pub
6 Essex St.
883-2150

Although it no longer hosts live music acts, the Essex Street Pub is one of Buffalo's cosiest corner bars. A favorite of the Buffalo artist set, the Pub offers a welcome diversion to Queen City painters, poets and musicians. A respectable beer selection and a warm, dark ambience make the Pub worth checking out.

The Funhouse / The Sideshow
1830 Abbott Rd.
Lacawanna
821-9150

A combination sports bar and dance club, the Funhouse is a suburban hot spot proudly boasting scantily-clad waitresses and a cross-section of top 40, heavy metal, classic rock, and dance music. The Sideshow, located in the rear of the building, hosts a healthy selection of national, international, and larger local acts. The Sideshow is the local outlet for Metropolitan Entertainment, so plenty of great shows pass through its doors. Dress is casual, and plenty of hair spray is encouraged for the ladies.

The Hard Rock Cafe
333 Prospect St.
Niagara Falls
282-0007

Although the food is unremarkable--essentially a Friday's in rocker's clothing--the beer selection at the Hard Rock is inviting, and the rock memorabilia collection well worth checking out. The staff is exceptionally friendly, the music always good, and occasionally, you can check out a local band on the week night, which is always a plus. Great location too--just minutes from the Falls and Casino Niagara. Recommended for the atmosphere and the beer selection.

Havana Fumidore
658 Main St.
849-0564

An upscale cigar bar, the Havana is paradise for cigar smokers, and problematic for non-smokers. Nice dress is encouraged, and martinis are to be reckoned with. Sporadically books live jazz. Recommended for smokers, its elegant decadence and the Theatre District location.

Jimmy Mac's
555 Elmwood Ave.
886-9112

(See : Restaurants)

Kingsnake Lounge
112 West Chippewa St.
856-3627

A relative newcomer to the Chippewa strip, the Kingsnake is a hip joint dedicated to an artsy, New York City ambience and a trendy urban stance. A variety of music both live and in-house, add to the atmosphere of wasted elegance. You'll hear jazz, swing, blues, and house rhythms on any given night of the week. Attire runs from casual to elegant. Highly recommended.

Lafayette Tap Room
320 Pearl St.
855-8800

A Buffalo landmark, and a club renowned throughout the country by blues connoisseurs, the Tap Room is a beautiful two-floor establishment that books the best in local, national and international blues talent. A great place to go for dinner and a few drinks on the first floor, followed by a night of rollicking tunes, dancing and partying on the second floor. Buffalonians are proud of this place, as they should be.

Left Bank
511 Rhode Island St.
882-3509

One of the nicest restaurants in the downtown area, the Left Bank also plays host to the arts crowd in the evenings. A good place to hear coffeehouse intellectuals holding forth on any given number of topics over an expensive bottle of wine at one of the many elegant but simply adorned tables, or musicians crying the independent artist blues over a cold bottle of Canadian beer at the bar. Not to be missed. *(See also: Restaurants)*

Merlin's
727 Elmwood Ave.
886-9270

A musician's bar of the first order, Merlin's makes up for in charm what it lacks in ritziness. Many of the city's musicians can be found here sitting at an open mike, checking out some fresh talent, tipping back a few pints at the patio bar, or indulging in fresh clams at the clam bar. No pretensions or attitudes at Merlin's, just a low-key good time.

Mr. Goodbar
1110 Elmwood Ave.
882-4000

A cool rock room with a great beer selection, including its own micro brew, plenty of space to spread out over two floors, an upstairs coffee bar, and patio seating right on the sidewalk of Elmwood Avenue in the summer. Goodbar is home to many of the college students attending Buffalo State College and University of Buffalo. A great spot to hear Buffalo bands ranging from hippie jams to punk rock. An enjoyable place to spend a Friday night with a drink and a friend.

Mohawk Place
47 East Mohawk St.
885-3931

Mohawk Place is one of the coolest bars in town. Not much to look at, certainly, but any Buffalonian club-hopper has at least a great memory or two from a night spent catching the best in regional and local blues, punk, alt-country and rockabilly at the Mohawk. A real "people" bar. Not to be missed.

Nietzsche's
248 Allen St.
886-8539

Nietzsche's is the only club in town dedicated to live original music 7 nights a week. Owner Joe Rubino and Co. brought us Ani DiFranco, The Tragically Hip, and countless others long before they were known to the masses. Nietzsche's is a cool bar with a real home-town friendly vibe. A favorite with Buffalonian musicians and music lovers for nearly two decades.

The Old Pink
Allen St. & Elmwood Ave.

A legendary night spot, the Old Pink is the cornerstone of the Allentown bar scene. Most evenings of clubbing end with a round or two at the Pink, a favorite of the under 40 Bohemian crowd. Famous for its grilled chicken sandwiches, cooked right behind the bar, The Pink is probably the coolest joint in town. DJ's spin the best in power-pop, rock-n-roll, and alternative music. Highly recommended.

Pearl Street Grill & Brewery/Cellar Bar
76 Pearl St.
856-2337

The Cellar bar is to Buffalo what the Cavern was to Liverpool; the spot to catch the best in local original music in a real rock-n-roll atmosphere. Upstairs, the Pearl Street Grill and Brewery *(see also: Restaurants)* offers an award winning array of brews, as well as fine American cuisine in a comfortable urban barroom setting. One could start with dinner on the second floor and end with a rockin' party in the basement. One of the brightest spots in the downtown area.

The Rendezvous
520 Niagara St.
849-1349

The current hottest hipster gathering point in Buffalo, this decades-old bar which recently reopened after a long convalescence is the place to be on weekend evenings. Nothing special about the beers, although a few specialty mixed drinks, some of which have survived from the 50's, spice up the drink menu. A guaranteed good time.

Shannon Pub
5050 Main Street
839-0002

The best Guiness in town is served at this fairly authentic Irish pub. A warm, cozy atmosphere pervades the dimly-lit Shannon, which hosts live Celtic music on most evenings.

67 West
67 West Chippewa St.
842-0281

The Chippewa district is the hub of the bustling weekend scene. 67 West will be jammed full of partiers on a Thursday, Friday or Saturday night, and offers a hip watering hole atmosphere. Casual dress, cool tunes and cold drinks rule the night. On less busy evenings, the club is a good place to grab a quiet drink.

The Tralfamadore Cafe
100 Theatre Place
851-8725

Recently taken over by new management, The Tralf is another Buffalo legend, a club with a rich history and a dedication to the best in local, national and international talent. The club originally came to prominence as a jazz club, hosting everyone from Pat Metheney to Grover Washington and Chuck Mangione, but in recent years it has branched out. Now, the Tralf is also home to pop, rock, comedy and dinner theatre, as well as a healthy dose of jazz. A posh setting prevails, so bring plenty of bread with you-- the drinks ain't cheap. Tables are available on a first come, first serve basis, but latecomers will find plenty of room to party by the bar. The Tralf remains one of the hippest places in town.

Exploring

■

EXPLORING BUFFALO

In 1804, city planner Joseph Ellicott designed Niagara Square to serve as the hub of his radial street plan for the Village of Buffalo. Today, the social hub of the city lies along **Elmwood Avenue**. The two mile stretch of the Avenue from Allen to Forest Streets known as the Elmwood Strip is an eclectic blend of restaurants, shops and galleries. The historic **Allentown** neighborhood (between Elmwood and Main Street, south of North St.) is full of restored 19th century homes. To the north, a lively mix of businesses can be found along **Hertel Avenue** with the highest concentration of shops located between Delaware and Starin Avenues. **Downtown** Buffalo *(see map next page)* remains primarily a business center, although the Main Place Mall offers shopping during the day while the Theatre District along Main Street and the Chippewa District *(see: Nightlife)* keep things alive in the evenings.

Architectural Sights

Downtown:
City Hall
65 Niagara Square
Prudential Building
28 Church St.
Ellicott Square
295 Main St.
Market Arcade
617 Main St.
St. Paul's Cathedral
Church at Pearl Sts.

North:
Buffalo Psychiatric Center
400 Forest Ave.

With so many buildings of historical significance in Buffalo, *New York Times* columnist RW Apple Jr. remarked, "You could do worse than take it [Buffalo] as a textbook for a course in modern American buildings." Designs by America's greatest architects, H.H. Richardson, Louis Sullivan and Frank Lloyd Wright, can be found in Buffalo. Richardson's Buffalo State Hospital (now the Psychiatric Center) with its twin towers of Medina sandstone was his first foray into the Romanesque Revival, a style that would later define his career. Sullivan's Prudential Building, an early steel-framed skyscraper is considered a masterwork with its graceful lines and elegant ornamentation. Sullivan's former drafter, Frank Lloyd Wright left a legacy of homes in Buffalo *(see page 93)*. Neighborhoods in which to begin exploring Buffalo's architecture include these: downtown, with the City Hall, Market Arcade, St. Paul's Episcopal Cathedral and the Ellicott Square Building among others; Allentown's quaint streets of restored Victorian homes; and Delaware Avenue from North to Bryant Streets-- a grand boulevard of 19th century mansions. In

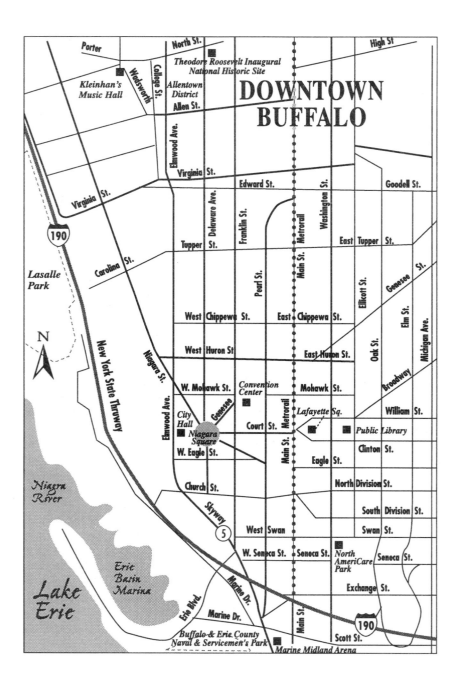

East:
New York Central
Terminal
Memorial & Paderewski
Drives

addition, the grain silos along the Buffalo River *(see page 94)* have a unique place in American architectural history.

Architectural
Walking Tours

Architectural walking tours, both self-guided and group, are offered from the Theodore Roosevelt Inaugural National Historic Site (884-0095). Areas include Allentown, downtown and Delaware Avenue. Informational audio tapes are provided for a small fee. The pamphlet, *Walk Buffalo,* available at the Visitors Center *(617 Main Street),* is an excellent guide to historic downtown Buffalo.

Buffalo and Erie
County Botanical
Gardens
2655 South Park Ave.
Daily
696-3555
☞**KIDS**

From under the large glass domes of this beautiful Victorian-style conservatory in South Park, grows the flora of environments from around the world. Built in the late 1890's as part of famed landscape architect Frederick Law Olmsted's master plan for Buffalo, the Conservatory is comprised of several interconnected areas. Upon entering, visitors approach the central dome, rising 67 feet above the collection of palm trees from the Americas, Pacific Islands and the Mediterranean. Other areas range from the high humidity room of ferns and tropical plants to the arid environment of the cacti. Trees and plants bearing edible fruits are also displayed. The Show House features seasonal exhibits such as the poinsettia display in December.

☞**NEARBY:**   *Restaurants: Blackthorn, Curly's.*

Broadway Market
999 Broadway
Mon.-Sat.
893-0705

Since the late 1800's this neighborhood has been the home to Buffalo's market. The current building, the third market structure on this site, was built in 1956. Ethnic foods, meats, produce, and baked goods are offered by the nearly fifty vendors.

Buffalo Zoological Gardens
300 Parkside Ave
Daily
837-3900
⊜**KIDS**

In 1870, when Buffalo mayor William F. Rogers received two deer as a gift, he sent them to graze in an area which would soon become the Buffalo Zoo. Today the Zoo covers over 23 acres of Delaware Park, and holds over 1000 animals from around the world. Although much of the Zoo was constructed during the 1930's under the WPA, many of the habitats have been rebuilt to reflect the trend toward larger, more naturalistic environments. Some of the rare and endangered species that the Zoo holds include a white tiger, Indian rhinos and a red panda. The Zoo offers numerous activities for children and the World of Wildlife Interactive Center provides hands on educational exhibits.

☞**NEARBY:** *Restaurants: Hutch's, Oliver's, Osaka, Park Lane.*

City Hall Observation Tower
Niagara Square
851-5991
Mon.-Fri.

Climb (or take the elevator, then climb) to the top of this Art Deco monster that hovers over Niagara Square. Great view of Lake Erie.

Delaware Park
Parkside Ave.,
Nottingham Ter. &
Elmwood Ave.
⊜**KIDS**

Frederick Law Olmsted, designer of New York City's Central Park and the most famous landscape architect in U.S. history, developed Buffalo's park system between 1868 and 1898. At the center of his plan was "The Park" a 350 acre rural area, that is now called Delaware Park.

Today the park is a popular spot to find walkers, joggers or those seeking tranquillity. There are also picnic facilities, tennis courts and an 18-hole golf course. Paddle boat rental on Hoyt Lake is available, weather permitting, May through October from 1pm to 8pm (882-5920).

Forest Lawn Cemetery and Garden Mausoleums
1411 Delaware Ave.
Daily
885-1600

What began in 1849 as an answer to both the burgeoning population of Buffalo and the prior year's cholera epidemic, is now one of the largest and most beautiful rural cemeteries in the country. The idea of rural cemeteries began as an outgrowth of the Romantic movement in Europe. Cemeteries would no longer be crowded adjuncts to churches, but natural sanctuaries, where art and nature would be united to provide a resting place for the dead as well as a contemplative park for the living. Forest Lawn Cemetery's glacier-carved landscape covers 269 acres and is home to over 144,000 permanent residents. The natural beauty of the Cemetery includes placid Mirror Lake, winding Scajaquada Creek, over 240 types of birds and Western New York's largest arboretum with over 10,000 trees. The artistic element of Forest Lawn is evidenced in the spectacular collection of funerary architecture. The list of notables buried at Forest Lawn is a long one and includes President Millard Fillmore, polar explorer Frederick Cook, General US Grant's Military Secretary Ely S. Parker and Seneca orator Red Jacket. The Cemetery is listed on the National Register of Historic Places.

Frank Lloyd Wright Houses
125 Jewett Parkway
118 Summit Ave.
285 Woodward Ave.

One of the most influential architects of the 20th Century, Frank Lloyd Wright built four houses, one cottage and an office building in Buffalo. Of the remaining structures the Darwin D. Martin Estate is the most significant. A prime example

also:
76 Soldier's Place
57 Tillinghast Place

of his Prairie Style, the estate is unique because it consists of three interconnected structures: the Darwin D. Martin House on Jewett Parkway, the George Barton House on Summit Avenue and a Gardener's Cottage on Woodward Avenue. Although the estate has been marred by the intrusion of an apartment complex, when the current restoration project is completed, it will help secure the future of an important piece of Buffalo architecture. Other Wright houses include the Walter V. Davidson House on Tillinghast Place and William R. Heath House on Soldier's Place. One of Wright's most significant designs, the Larkin Administration Building was razed in 1950.

Grain Elevators
Ohio St. to Childs St.

These imposing concrete edifices along the Buffalo River, an eyesore to some, stand not only as a reminder of 19th Century Buffalo, but as a historical footnote to the progress of 20th Century architecture. Although concrete grain silos were first built in Minneapolis, it was these Buffalo grain elevators that would gain unexpected renown. When illustrations of Buffalo's General Mills and Concrete Central elevators were published in Europe between 1913 and 1930, they served to influence revolutionary modern architects like Frenchman Le Corbusier and Bauhaus school founder Walter Gropius. The elevators' soaring windowless shapes along with the seamless concrete exterior and massive scale, made them the forerunners of the modern skyscraper. For a unique tour of Buffalo's industrial past try navigating the Buffalo river on the Urban Canoe Trail *(see: Boating, this chapter).*

Naval & Military Park

1 Naval Park Cove
April-Oct. Daily
Nov. Sat. & Sun. only
847-6405
☞**KIDS**

This waterfront park stands as a tribute to veterans from all branches of the Armed Forces. Visitors can climb aboard and explore three naval vessels: the guided missile cruiser USS Little Rock, the destroyer USS The Sullivans and the decorated submarine USS Croaker which sunk eleven Japanese vessels during the Pacific campaign of 1944-1945. The enormous size of these vessels is easily overlooked while experiencing the cramped living quarters of World War II servicemen. The park also displays aircraft, land and amphibious vehicles, and weaponry such as mines and depth charges. There are also exhibits and memorabilia dedicated to Polish Forces, Korean War Veterans and US Marines.

☞**NEARBY:** *Restaurant: Pearl Street Grill.*

Our Lady of Victory National Shrine and Basilica

767 Ridge Rd.
Lackawanna
Daily
823-2490
tours: 828-9444

Our Lady of Victory, the second church in the United States to be given the Papal distinction of Basilica, with its 165 feet high twin towers topped by copper angels, majestically presides over the city of Lackawanna. The Basilica exists due to the devotion of Father Nelson H. Baker, whose work helped turn the steel town into the "City of Charity."Built in the Italian Renaissance style and completed in 1926, the enormous scale of the building becomes more evident upon entering. Along the outside walls, carved from single blocks of marble, are life-sized scenes of the Stations of the Cross. The tremendous ceiling panels and soaring central dome are adorned by the painting of noted Italian artist Gonippo Raggiare. Behind the altar stand massive twisted columns of red Pyrenees marble. Among the shrines is the unique Grotto Shrine, built with lava from Mt. Vesuvius.

☞**NEARBY:** *Restaurant: Curly's.*

QRS Music Rolls Inc.
1026 Niagara St.
Mon.-Fri.
Tours at 10am and 2pm
885-4600
☞**KIDS**

During the height of the "roaring twenties" when player pianos were all the rage, QRS manufactured as many as 11 million music rolls per year. Today, although sales have waned, this Buffalo factory remains the world's oldest and largest manufacturer of player piano rolls. Tours begin with a short slide presentation before proceeding into the factory. Of particular interest is the exhibit of a 1917 "Marking Piano," the only one in existence. This revolutionary device allowed noted artists, like ragtime pianist Charlie Straight and jazz composer Fats Waller, to record their performances for roll production. The rolls of these original performances along with more contemporary pieces, comprise part of the factory's extensive inventory.

Theodore Roosevelt Inaugural National Historical Site
641 Delaware Ave.
Parking off Franklin St.
Daily
Closed Saturdays from January - March
884-0095

One of only five inaugural sites outside of Washington D.C., the stately home that overlooks Delaware Avenue was where Theodore Roosevelt became president in 1901. The building originally served as the officers' headquarters for the Buffalo Barracks, a garrison constructed in 1837 to defend early Buffalo from a possible war with Canada. By 1901, when President McKinley was assassinated in Buffalo, the home was the private residence of prominent lawyer and longtime Roosevelt friend, Ansley Wilcox and his family. It was in the Wilcox's library that Roosevelt was sworn-in after rushing back to Buffalo from a vacation in the Adirondacks. The museum details the events of the assassination and contains artifacts pertinent to the transition period. One such item is the singed handkerchief in which assassin Leon Czolgosz concealed the gun he used to shoot McKinley.

☞**NEARBY:**   *Restaurants: Biac's, Enchanté, Fiddle Heads.*

Tifft Nature Preserve
1200 Fuhrmann Blvd.
Daily
Visitor's Center
Tues.-Sun.
825-6397
☞**KIDS**

The Tifft Preserve, a 264-acre nature refuge, is an interesting site not only because of its natural wonders, but due to its fascinating history. Once the dairy farm of prominent 19th century businessman George Washington Tifft, the parcel eventually became a docking area for ships transferring iron ore, coal and lumber. Left abandoned for many years, the City of Buffalo purchased the land in the 1970's as a dumping ground for almost two million cubic yards of solid waste. After a committee composed of concerned citizens, sportsmen and naturalists' organizations helped save the area's wetlands, the waste was trucked in and plowed into four huge mounds. Today, the preserve, operated by the Buffalo Museum of Science, provides a habitat for numerous plants and animals. Foremost among these is a large bird population. Over 250 species of birds have been recorded in and around the preserve. There are five miles of hiking trails and a 75-acre cattail marsh. During the winter, bring your cross-country skis or rent snowshoes at the center.

MUSEUMS

Amherst Museum
3755 Tonawanda Creek
Rd., Amherst
Apr.-Oct. Tues.-Sun.
Nov.-Mar. Tues.-Fri.
689-1440
☞**KIDS**

The Amherst Museum is dedicated to the exploration of 19th century life on the Niagara Frontier. Spread about the 35-acre historic park are restored houses, commercial buildings and two schoolhouses, all of which have been transplanted here from the Amherst area. Educational programs and craft guilds are designed to keep past skills and methods alive. The museum's indoor facility contains exhibits concerning domestic life, crafts and technology of the period. The Aviation Building features a unique Cunningham-Hall plane from 1936.

Buffalo and Erie County Historical Society
25 Nottingham Court
Tues.-Sun.
873-9644

The Historical Society makes its home in the only remaining building from the Pan-American Exposition of 1901. The museum showcases the sociological, industrial and cultural aspects of Buffalo and western New York through permanent and temporary exhibits. The Research Library (Wed.-Sat. 873-9612) contains thousands of books, photographs and manuscripts, among them, a number of President Fillmore's papers. The extensive genealogy resources are invaluable for those researching family trees.

Buffalo Museum of Science
1020 Humboldt Pkwy.
Tues.-Sun.
896-5200
Kellogg Observatory
Fridays (weather permitting)
Sept.-May
☞**KIDS**

The Buffalo Museum of Science is dedicated to presenting permanent and temporary exhibits relating to the natural sciences. Exhibits begin on the second floor and include examples of vertebrates and invertebrates, endangered species and flora. The Dinosaurs & Co. exhibit displays fossils pre-dating the age of the dinosaurs and also includes skeletons and skeletal casts of dinosaurs. The third floor displays a large collection of birds, the gem and mineral exhibit and a fascinating look at how zebra mussels can overrun a car pulled from the Buffalo Harbor. The fourth floor is devoted to the Hall of Space.

SHOPPING

In addition to the specialty shops and boutiques along the aforementioned Elmwood Strip and Hertel Avenue, a wide variety of shopping possibilities exist in Buffalo. The mall scene is represented by several area malls including Main Place Mall downtown, Boulevard Mall in Amherst, Eastern Hills on Transit Road, and the area's largest mall, Walden Galleria, just off Thruway exit 52. For the frugal shopper, the Niagara International Factory Outlets in Niagara Falls, NY, features over 150 designer outlets. Antique lovers can enjoy the many shops clustered in historic Allentown and on Hertel Avenue.

BOAT TOURS

ERIE CANAL TOURS

Considered one of the engineering marvels of its time (completed in 1825), the Erie Canal was instrumental in both the development of upstate cities as well as opening commerce to the expanding west. After years of neglect, the canal is experiencing a rebirth with paved trails where the mules once labored and tour boats in place of barges (see: *Day Trips, Lockport Locks and Erie Canal Cruises*). For more information on the New York State Canal System contact the NYS Canal Corporation at: (800) 422-6254.

NIAGARA RIVER & LAKE ERIE CRUISES

Grande Lady
Holiday Inn
100 Whitehaven Rd.
Grand Island
Reservations required
774-8594

The Grande Lady is an 80-foot yacht-style cruise vessel that has a 125 passenger capacity. Group charters can select from variety of routes and menus; dinner, brunch, lunch, and moonlight cruises are available.

Miss Buffalo II
79 Marine Dr.
Tues.-Sun.
June-September
856-6696

Cruises depart from near the Naval Park and travel up Lake Erie and along the Niagara River offering scenic views of the Buffalo skyline and Canadian Shore. Afternoon and evening tours.

Niagara Clipper
650 River Rd.
North Tonawanda, NY
Tues.-Sun.
May-October
856-6696

The Niagara Clipper cruises along the upper Niagara River from North Tonawanda. Lunch, brunch and dinner cruises are available.

OUTDOORS

BICYCLING

In addition to the miles of road riding, there are a number of bike trails in Western New York. For scenic views of the Niagara River there are the two Riverwalk Trails, one a 6.6 mile path that starts near the Erie Basin Marina and extends North along the Niagara River to beyond Squaw Island, the other a 3 mile trail along the Niagara in Tonawanda through Isle View Park. Other trails include the 5 mile Amherst Bike Path along Ellicott Creek and the Tonawanda Creek Trail along the Erie Canal near the Amherst Museum. For a longer Erie Canal ride, the Erie Canal Heritage Trail hugs the historic canal for 70-miles from Lockport to Fairport. The trail is part of the New York State Canalway Trail that, when completed, will span over 500 miles connecting Buffalo to the Hudson River while passing through numerous villages, cities and historic locks. A handy guide to biking the canal, the *Erie Canal Bicyclist and Hiker's Route Guide*, is available at bookstores. For group rides, Western New York's largest bicycle club, the Niagara Frontier Bicycle Club (www.NFBC.com) offers over 400 rides per season for all ages and abilities.

BOATING

With the proximity of two Great Lakes and the Niagara River, there is no shortage of waterways for boating in the Buffalo area. Public launch sites are available seasonally from May to October at The Aud Club Erie Basin Marina, 329 Erie Street, (842-4141); NFTA Small Boat Harbor Marina, 111 Fuhrmann Blvd., (852-1921) and South End Marina, Fuhrmann Blvd., (852-0333). The Tonawanda Launch at Sheridan Drive and River Road (831-1001) is open year-round. For a more urban adventure, the Buffalo River Urban Canoe Trail is a self guided tour of Buffalo's environmental and historical sites. A detailed trail guide is available for free from the Department of Environmental Conservation (851-7010). Two vital guides for boaters are *Ports Cruising Guide* and *Cruising Guide to New York Waterways and Lake Champlain.*

FISHING AND HUNTING

The combination of Lake Erie and the Niagara River provide the Buffalo area with some of the finest sport fishing in America, while hunters enjoy both the large and small game that is prevalent throughout Western New York. High concentrations of smallmouth bass and schools of walleye are reasons to fish

Lake Erie. In the Lake Erie tributaries (Buffalo River and Eighteenmile Creek) steelhead are plentiful, especially during Spring and Fall migrations. The upper Niagara River boasts the highest catch rate in the country for the huge muskellunge. The lower Niagara is a great place for steelhead, lake trout, chinook salmon, walleye and smallmouth bass. For information on what's biting call the Lake Erie fishing hotline 855-FISH or 679-ERIE. Deer hunting, a popular Western New York activity, is limited to 8 weeks each fall. The area features an abundance of small game, most within a half hour of the city. Species include grouse, rabbit, squirrel, woodcock, turkey and pheasant. The Niagara River provides hunters with tremendous numbers of waterfowl. For those looking for a more passive experience, the Department of Environmental Conservation offers several wildlife viewing areas throughout New York State. For information on hunting, fishing or wildlife viewing contact the DEC at 851-7010.

GOLF

The Buffalo area is home to many fine public and private golf courses. The following list represents a selection of Buffalo's best public courses.

Beaver Island
2136 West Oakfield Rd.
Grand Island, NY
773-4668

Located in Beaver Island State Park, this course has little or no rough, big fairways and greens. You'll find water and bunkers but nothing too tricky. Very reasonable greens fees.

Byrncliff Resort
Rte. 20A
Varysburg, NY
535-7300

This course has an excellent layout, and is especially beautiful during fall foliage colors. It's tougher than you may think and gives plenty of challenge. Reasonably priced.

Dande Farms
Carney Rd.
Akron, NY
542-2027

An 18-hole course with no bunkers. Long course with tree-lined fairways. Distance is the key to scoring well.

Deerwood Golf Course
1818 Sweeney Rd.
N. Tonawanda, NY
695-8525

The first hole is over 600 yards long and that sets the stage for a lengthy golf course. Reasonable greens fees, lots of length. Expanding from 18 to 27 holes, the new nine will bring a new and improved style of golf to Deerwood.

Elma Meadows
1711 Girdle Rd.
Elma, NY
652-5475

Golf in the country, not overly long, and if you hit it straight you should score well. Second hole stands out as a challenge through shoots of trees. Inexpensive.

Glen Oak
711 Smith Rd.
E. Amherst, NY
688-5454

This tremendous Robert Trent Jones design is both challenging and beautiful. Recently rejuvenated sand bunkers have made a great course even better. Kart mandatory facility.

Rothland
12089 Clarence Cent. Rd.
Akron, NY
542-4325

Of the twenty-seven holes, the gold nine are the best of the three sets. Good layout, plenty of trees and water. A good iron player will benefit and score well.

Sheridan Park
Sheridan Drive
Tonawanda, NY
875-1811

Arguably the best starting hole in Western NY. Not always in great condition, but can be a good test, especially the long par 4's.

Willowbrook
Rte. 98
Lockport, NY
434-0111

Back 9 is a shotmaker's special, short and tight. Every hole is carved by tree-lined fairways and it's necessary to hit the ball straight. Numerous shoots of trees, keep your driver in the bag.

A SHORT "DRIVE"

Batavia Country Club
7909 Batavia-Byron Rd.
Batavia, NY
343-7600

Course is in best shape ever and getting better. Layout includes nice rolling hills. Inexpensive golf.

Chestnut Hill
1330 Broadway
Darien, NY
547-9699

Always in great shape, can be challenging, large greens and tees, good golfing value. Specializes in tournaments.

Peek'n Peak
(Upper Course)
1405 Olde Road
Clymer, NY 355-4141

Unlike anything in Western NY, this young course features elevation changes and fantastic views. A test at every hole, high-end greens fees, but worth it.

Terry Hills
Rte. 33
Batavia, NY
(800) 825-8633

Not overly long, a great shot maker's course with 27 holes, rolling hills. Excellent condition and great service from the Rotondo family.

OTHER AREA PUBLIC GOLF COURSES

Amherst Audubon
500 Maple Rd.
Williamsville, NY
631-7139

Amherst Oakwood
Tonawanda Creek Rd.
Amherst NY
689-1421

Bob-O-Link
4085 Transit Rd.
Orchard Park, NY
662-4311

Bright Meadows
12287 Clarence Rd.
Akron, NY
542-2441

Brighton Park
Brompton Rd.
Tonawanda, NY
695-2580

Cazenovia Golf Course
Wildwood Pl.
825-9811

Delaware Golf Course
Delaware Park
835-2533

Eden Valley Golf Course
10401 Sisson Highway
Eden, NY
337-2190

Evergreen Golf Club
100 Tonawanda Creek Rd.
West Amherst, NY
688-6204

Grandview Golf Course
444 Central Ave.
Angola, NY
549-4930

Greenwood Golf Course
8499 Northfield Rd.
Clarence Center, NY
741-3395

Grover Cleveland
3781 Main St.
Amherst, NY
862-9470

Hamburg Golf Course
Boston State Rd.
Hamburg, NY
648-4410

Holland Hills County Club
10438 Holland-Glenwood Rd.
Glenwood, NY
537-2345

Pine Meadows Golf Club
9820 Greiner Rd.
Clarence, NY
741-3970

South Park Golf Course
2539 South Park Ave.
825-9504

South Shore Country Club
5076 Southwester Blvd.
Hamburg, NY
649-6674

HIKING

Hiking in western New York ranges from short day hikes in area parks (see below) to longer treks along the Finger Lakes Trail, which when completed, will connect the Catskills with the Allegheny Mountains as it passes through the Southern Tier of New York State. The Niagara Trail System, a series of small trail sections that parallel the Niagara River Gorge, allow a close view of the geological history of the gorge along with the flora and fauna, and lucky hikers may catch a glimpse of a bald eagle. Additional wildlife watching can be enjoyed at one of the state's wildlife viewing areas *(see: Fishing and Hunting)*. The Dr. Victor Reinstein Woods Nature Preserve in the town of Cheektowaga (683-5959) consists of 285 acres of undisturbed forest and wetlands. Access to the preserve is limited to guided tours. Nearby areas for day hikes include: Erie County Forest in the southeast corner of Erie County, Hunter Creek Park near East Aurora, and near Medina there's the Iroquois National Wildlife Refuge, along with the Oak Orchard and Tonawanda State Wildlife Management Areas. The book, *Fifty Hikes in Western New York,* is a good source for additional hiking opportunities. For backpackers, to the south there's Allegheny National Forest and for more expansive terrain, the Adirondack Forest Preserve's three million acres are about 4 hours away.

PARKS

Western New York has thousands of acres of parkland in which to enjoy a variety of activities. In the summer there's picnicking, softball, tennis, hiking, fishing and swimming while the winter brings, cross-county and downhill skiing, snowmobiling, and skating. Information regarding city parks is available from the Parks Department at: 851-5806. In addition to the city parks, the Erie County Parks system consists of seven major parks: Akron Falls, Chestnut Ridge, Como, Ellicott Creek, Emery, Isle View and Sprague Brook. For more information contact the Erie County Parks Department at: 858-8355. State parks provide more recreational opportunities including camping. To make camping reservations call: (800) 456-2267.

SKIING

Those who malign Buffalo for its winter weather need to get out of the house and strap on a pair of skis. Cross-country terrain is abundant in all of the Erie County parks and at private areas like Byrncliff Resort, 13 miles east of East Aurora in Varysburg (535-7300). If there's not enough snow on the ground, local downhill areas produce enough of the man-made version to extend the season from approximately early December until April. For ski conditions call: (800)-367-9691.

Chestnut Ridge
6121 Chestnut Ridge Rd.
Orchard Park, NY
662-3290

Vertical Drop: 200 feet
Terrain: 2 slopes and trails
Lifts: 1 tow bar
Small learners' hill for alpine skiing, cross-county area, ice skating, sledding. Free.

Cokaigne Ski Center
1493 County Road 66
Cherry Creek, NY
287-3223

Vertical Drop: 430 feet
Terrain: 15 slopes and trails.
Lifts: 3 Double Chairs, 1 J-bar
Night skiing, boarding half-pipe.

Holiday Valley
Route 219
Ellicottville, NY
699-2345

Vertical Drop: 750 feet
Terrain: 52 slopes and trails.
Lifts: 10 chair lifts, two tows.
Night skiing, boarding, Nordic trails, day care.

HoliMont
Rte.242
Ellicottville, NY
699-2320
Conditions: 699-4720

Vertical Drop: 620
Terrain: 45 slopes and trails
Lifts: 7 chair lifts and 2 tows
Private area that accepts non-members weekdays only, boarding half-pipe, Nordic trail.

Kissing Bridge
Route 240
Glenwood, NY
592-4963
Conditions: 592-4961

Vertical Drop: 600 feet
Terrain: 36 slopes and trails
Lifts: 6 chair lifts and 4 tows
Night skiing, boarding half-pipe, tubing area, day care.

Peek'n Peak
1405 Olde Rd.
Clymer, NY
355-4141

Vertical Drop: 400 feet
Terrain: 27 slopes and trails
Lifts: 9 chair lifts
Night skiing, tubing, boarding, Nordic terrain.

Ski Tamarack
7414 State Rd.
Colden, NY
941-6821

Vertical Drop: 500 feet
Terrain: 15 slopes and trails
Lifts: 1 chair lift and 2 tows
Thursday through Sunday only, Night skiing, boarding.

SPECTATOR SPORTS

One thing that's impossible to ignore about living in Buffalo is the importance the city places on its sports teams. In addition to the beloved football Bills, Buffalo fans enthusiastically support the National Hockey League's Sabres, the indoor lacrosse Bandits and the Triple "A" baseball Bisons. The Marine Midland Arena hosts the Sabres along with the Arena football Destroyers and the indoor soccer Blizzard. The Bills are home in Orchard Park and the Bisons play in downtown's beautiful North Americare Park. Fans of harness Racing can travel to **Buffalo Raceway** (649-1280) in Hamburg.

Tickets: **Bandits and Sabres:** 855-4100
Bills: 649-0015
Bisons: 846-2000
Blizzard: 855-4400
Destroyers: 881-4444

The Arts

ART MUSEUMS

Albright-Knox Art Gallery
1285 Elmwood Ave.
Tues.-Sun.
882-8700

Housed inside an imposing Greek Revival building and its modern addition is one of the richest collections of contemporary art in the country. Much of the gallery's renown has come from the quality and depth of works from the artists of the second half of the twentieth century. However, the gallery also displays a fine collection of painting and sculpture from every major period in history. The collection stretches from early Asian objects to a strong Impressionist and Post Impressionist collection that includes the works of Cézanne, Degas, Monet and vanGogh. The movements of the early part of the following century are also well represented by artists such as Kandinsky, Matisse, Miró, and Picasso. In addition to its permanent collection, the gallery presents a number of special exhibitions throughout the year.

☞**NEARBY:**   *Restaurants: (See Elmwood Strip page 8)*

Burchfield-Penney Art Center
Buffalo State College
1300 Elmwood Ave.
Tues.-Sun.
878-6003

The Arts Center, on the campus of SUNY Buffalo, is dedicated to promoting and preserving works from western New York artists and craftsmen. The Center is named in part, for Charles E. Burchfield (1893-1967) who began as a wallpaper designer and eventually became one of the country's most respected watercolorists. The Burchfield-Penney holds the largest public collection of his paintings along with drawings, prints, sketches, journals and studio equipment. Also on exhibit are the works of Burchfield's contemporaries, including the sculpture of Charles Cary Rumsey. The Center's Roycroft exhibit showcases the furniture, books and other objects created as part of the Arts and Crafts movement by Elbert Hubbard's community in East Aurora. Changing exhibits every two months.

Cofeld Judaic Museum of Temple Beth Zion
805 Delaware Ave.
Mon.-Sat.
886-7150

This small museum showcases thousands of Judaic artifacts collected from around the world. Both religious and cultural artifacts are on display dating back to the 10th century.

ART GALLERIES

NON-PROFIT GALLERIES

Art Dialogue Gallery/ Western New York Artists Group
1 Linwood Ave.
Tues.-Sat.
885-2251

The non-profit Western New York Artists Group works in conjunction with the Art Dialogue Gallery to present exhibitions that primarily encompass works from Western New York artists. The group is comprised of over 200 artist members and produces more than twenty shows annually.

Big Orbit Gallery
30D Essex Street
Thurs.-Sun.
883-3209

Big Orbit Gallery is dedicated to presenting works in all media from emerging artists, all of whom have ties to Western New York. Big Orbit's space has a rich history in Buffalo's art community. The former ice packing complex was once the home of CEPA Gallery, Hallwalls and the Artists Gallery. The area that at one time served as Hallwalls' performance space is now home to seven or eight exhibitions per year, including both solo and group shows. Works from the Gallery's three hundred members are showcased at the annual members' show.

Buffalo Arts Studio
Tri-Main Building
2495 Main St.
Suite 500
Tues.-Fri.
833-4450

By providing artists with a studio in which to work, and by helping to expose their works, the Buffalo Art Studio has become a vital institution both to area artists, and the greater community. Located on the third and fifth floors of the Tri-Main Center, the studio represents over 70 artists and exhibits works from regional, national and international artists. The group's community outreach program has been responsible for creating murals, sculptures and gardens throughout the community by teaming artists with disadvantaged children.

CEPA Gallery
617 Main St.
Tues.-Sun.
856-2717

The Center for Exploratory and Perceptual Art, began in 1974 and has grown to one of the largest and best equipped centers for the visual arts in the country. Focusing on photography, film and digital art, CEPA's newest home is in the Market Arcade downtown. Several exhibitions are presented each year spread throughout the three galleries that span various levels of the Arcade. In addition to showcasing local, national and international artists' works, CEPA's educational programs offer training for children and adults. The educational facilities include a teaching darkroom and a digital-imaging laboratory.

El Museo Francisco Oller y Diego Rivera
91 Allen St.
Mon.-Fri.
884-9693

El Museo began as a Latino gallery, but is now dedicated to promoting and exhibiting works from all minority artists. Over the years, much of the Gallery's work could be found throughout the community, but the new space on Allen Street provides a permanent home in which to hold exhibitions.

**Fanette Goldman/
Carolyn Greenfield
Art Gallery**
Daemen College
4380 Main St.
Mon.-Sat.
839-8241

On the campus of Daemen College, the Goldman/Greenfield Gallery offers students an opportunity to learn through visiting artists' works. Along with the three to five outside shows per year, the gallery presents student and faculty shows and the popular High School exhibition.

Gallery 81
81 Allen St.
Daily
867-8881

This Allentown gallery is devoted to exhibiting paintings from area artists. The four or five shows per year focus primarily on contemporary, modern and graffiti art.

**Hallwalls
Contemporary Art
Center**
Tri-Main Building
2495 Main St.
Tues.-Fri.
835-7362

Inspired by some of the artist-run alternative organizations that were opening in cities during the late 1960's and 70's, Hallwalls was established in 1974 as the Asford Hollow Foundation. During the next twenty-five years, through exhibition and performance, the Center gained national prominence as one of the leading venues for alternative artists. Now located on the fourth floor of the Tri-Main Center, Hallwalls promotes the visual arts (painting, sculpture, film, theater) music, and writing through exhibitions, performance, and workshops.

Impact Artists Gallery
Tri-Main Building
2495 Main St.
Tues.-Fri.
835-6817

Impact Artists Gallery, is a cooperative gallery that provides opportunities for women in the arts. Now located in the Tri-Main Building, Impact presents changing shows monthly in every media. In addition, the gallery serves as a meeting place for women's cultural organizations, business and support groups, workshops and classes.

Squeaky Wheel
175 Elmwood Ave.
Mon.-Fri.
884-7172

Squeaky Wheel is a non-profit arts center dedicated to the promotion of audio, computer, film and video art. The center offers workshops for children and adults, produces both a magazine and a cable access program, and exhibits works from regional and national artists. Equipment rental is also available.

**UB Art Gallery &
Art Department
Gallery**
Center for the Arts
University at Buffalo
Amherst Campus
Tues.-Sat.
645-2626

Located in the University at Buffalo's Center for the Arts, the UB Art Gallery focuses on contemporary works by national and international artists. The Art Department Gallery also exhibits the artwork of students and faculty members.

**Villa Maria College
Gallery**
Mon.-Sat.
240 Pine Ridge Rd.
896-0700

This college gallery presents about eight shows per year in a variety of media. Local, regional and nationally prominent artists are featured. Student and faculty exhibitions are also showcased.

COMMERCIAL GALLERIES

Anderson Gallery
Martha Jackson Place
Tues.-Sat.
Closed August
834-2579

In 1953, when Martha Jackson opened her first gallery in New York City, the concept of showing and selling contemporary American works was seen by many as folly. But with an acute knowledge of art, an unwavering support for the artists that she represented and a devotion to their vision, she helped change the way the world viewed contemporary art. By integrating European and Asian shows with modern American works and by introducing American works to Europe, Jackson helped form a bridge between the continents that helped internationalize the art world. After her death in 1969, the Gallery was headed by her son, David Anderson, who in 1987 decided to relocate in Buffalo. In 1991, the Gallery's present home, a renovated former elementary school, opened. Although no longer representing individual artists, the Anderson Gallery remains committed to the promotion of modern and contemporary art by its presentation of five or six shows per year.

Arnak Art Gallery
255 Great Arrow St.
Mon-Fri.
874-8873

Now located in the former Pierce Arrow building, Arnak was established in 1978 as a Gallery for Inuit and Native American works. Although the Gallery still has the largest collection of such art in Western New York, they have since expanded their scope to include works from local, national and international artists. Home and corporate consulting, appraisal and custom framing are available.

Artisan's Gallery & Gift Shop
1472 Hertel Ave.
Mon.-Sat.
836-2706

This little shop on Hertel sells original artwork and handcrafted items. A popular spot for gifts, Artisan's carries fine art, hand-woven textiles, pottery, glass and jewelry.

Benjaman's Art Gallery
419 Elmwood Ave.
Mon.& Tues.
Thurs.-Sat.
886-0898

Wander through this old house on Elmwood that is literally filled to the attic with artwork. Established over 25 years ago, Benjaman's has a huge inventory of fine art and posters. Works are displayed throughout three floors, from the sun porch to the bathroom. Large selection of Erté and Buffalo's Jimmy Litz. Framing, restoration and appraisals are offered.

Brian Art Galleries
717 Elmwood Ave.
Tues.-Sat.
883-7599

A storefront gallery on Elmwood that focuses primarily on contemporary works in the form of limited edition prints and watercolors. Regional, national and international artists are represented. Established in 1980, the gallery also offers corporate and residential consultation.

College St. Gallery
82 College St.
Fri.-Mon.
882-9727

Director Michael Mulley, who holds a degree in Fine Arts Photography, operates this tiny Allentown gallery. The one-time barbershop now houses works in all media with an emphasis on photography. There is also a wide selection of original rock, jazz and blues photographs.

Dana Tillou Fine Arts
417 Franklin St.
Wed.-Sat.
854-5285

For a commercial gallery to thrive for over thirty years in the same location is a major feat, but Dana Tillou has accomplished just that. The stately building on the corner of Franklin and Virginia houses three showrooms of art and antiques. The Gallery deals in works from the 18th to the early part of the twentieth century and includes some early regional pieces. Appraising and research are also available.

Fineline Gallery
1599 Hertel Ave.
Mon.-Sat.
838-4411

Former University of Buffalo professor and artist Bert Grobe, operates this North Buffalo gallery. Fineline is strongly committed to the promotion of early 20th century regional art through both educational means and by exhibiting works. The gallery presents about six shows per year and also deals in antiques.

Nina Freudenheim
Hotel Lenox
140 North St.
Mon.-Fri.
882-5777

A long established and well known gallery that represents numerous artists of national and international prominence. The gallery focuses on contemporary fine art and presents four exhibits per year.

Vern Stein Fine Art
5747 Main St.
Williamsville
Tues.-Sat.
626-5688

Works from the late 19th century to the present are on display at this Willamsville gallery. Much of the gallery is dedicated to antique paintings and prints. The contemporary pieces also reflect a more traditional style. Consultation and appraisal are available.

MUSIC

Ars Nova Musicians Chamber Orchestra
896-2515 or 662-3598

Ars Nova is dedicated to the performance of chamber music ranging from the Baroque period to contemporary pieces. The group is led by Music Director/Conductor Marylouise Nanna and is primarily comprised of members of the Buffalo Philharmonic Orchestra. The annual Viva Vivaldi Festival during the first four Sundays in November highlights Vivaldi's chamber pieces along with works from other "vicarious visionaries." The festival takes place in select Buffalo churches and therefore not only sheds a spotlight on local talent, but helps expose some of the architecturally significant churches in Buffalo.

Buffalo Chamber Music Society
838-2383

For over 75 years the Chamber Music Society has been presenting concerts in various venues around Buffalo including the acoustically superior Mary Seaton Room at Kleinhans Music Hall. Performances include nationally and internationally known soloists, trios and quartets.

Buffalo Philharmonic Chorus
447-1927

Originally founded as the Buffalo Schola Cantorum, this 120 member chorus serves primarily as the choral ensemble for the Philharmonic Orchestra's productions. The independent chorus also performs in area churches, along with summer shows at Artpark and Chautauqua Institution.

Buffalo Philharmonic Orchestra
Kleinhans Music Hall
885-5000

Since its opening season in 1935, the Buffalo Philharmonic Orchestra has been one of the most important cultural institutions in western New York. Over the years the orchestra has performed with the worlds' great soloists and has been conducted by such luminaries as Stravinsky, Bernstein and Marriner. In addition to the concert series at Kleinhans, the orchestra presents several community and youth concerts each year. The Pops series is lead by trumpeter Doc Severinsen.

Buffalo Suzuki Strings
876-0710

Patterned after Dr. Shinichi Suzuki's educational philosophy, the Buffalo Suzuki strings has been teaching and presenting concerts since 1969. Public performances are staged throughout the community as well as at private functions.

Erie County Wind Ensemble
625-8754

The Erie County Wind Ensemble was founded in 1983 as a group composed primarily of music teachers. Currently under the baton of John Maguda, the forty-four member ensemble consists of fine players from various backgrounds dedicated to performing the best of wind literature. About ten performances are held throughout the community per year.

DANCE

Buffalo City Ballet
Rockwell Hall
Buffalo State College
tickets: 878-3005

Buffalo City Ballet is a resident company that explores various choreographic styles with an emphasis on classical ballet. Their season is from September to May and classes are available.

Buffalo Contemporary Dance
882-0796

Buffalo Contemporary Dance is a new company founded by dance professionals that have either taught or performed in Western NY over the years. Performances incorporate multi-media effects, and live music and include ensemble , solo and duet pieces.

Kakilambe Dance & Drum Performing Troupe
884-2013

Part of the African-American Cultural Center, Kakilambe is a repertory dance company specializing in African dance. The troupe was founded in 1958, becoming the first Black dance company in Buffalo. In addition to performing traditional African dance, the troupe produces works originating from the Caribbean and Haiti.

Pick of the Crop Dance
Glenn & Awdrey Flickinger Performing Arts Center
Nichols School
1250 Amherst St.
881-3824

Founded in 1991 by choreographer/dancer Elaine Gardner and composer/musician Curt Steinzor, Pick of the Crop Dance is a modern dance company that places an emphasis on performing new works. In addition to pieces by Gardner and others, each season the resident company works with a commissioned choreographer to produce a new work. Original music and unique set pieces often accompany the performances. Along with its home season at the Flickinger Center, the company tours extensively throughout the area and provides educational opportunities in the form of workshops, lectures, youth collaborations, and school performances.

Zodiaque Dance Company
U.B. Center for the Arts
645-6898

Although Zodiaque is the resident dance company at the University of Buffalo, it is not simply a student company. The inclusion of teachers, and professional-level adult students elevate the quality of performance and bring a versatility of experience that allows the group to produce pieces in all forms of dance. Their season runs from September to May and includes touring.

THEATER

Alleyway Theatre
1 Curtain Up Alley
852-2600

The Alleyway Theatre is one of only a handful of theaters in the country devoted solely to presenting new works. Productions are chosen from an international competition and winning playwrights are brought to town to aid in the creative process. Two premieres are staged in the spring, two in the fall and a festival of new short plays each June.

Buffalo Ensemble Theatre
New Phoenix Theatre
95 North Johnson Pkwy.
855-2225

Buffalo Ensemble Theatre (BET) is a fully professional theatre that focuses on producing contemporary and new drama. Founded over 20 years ago, BET's seven play season runs from September to June.

Buffalo United Artists
884 Main St.
886-9239

Buffalo United Artists, more commonly referred to as BUA, is a professional theatre group whose mission is to use theatre as a vehicle for social change. After several years of performing in various theaters, BUA has recently found a permanent home on Main Street between Virginia and Allen Streets.

Irish Classical Theatre Company
The Andrews Theatre
625 Main St.
853-4282

As the name implies, Irish Classical Theatre Company focuses primarily on works by Irish playwrights, although the repertoire also includes international classics. The company's new space, a 200 seat theatre in the round, is a result of their fast growing popularity and reputation for high quality productions. The five-play season runs from September to May.

The Kavinoky Theatre
320 Porter Ave.
881-7668

The Kavinoky Theatre stages five shows each season from September to May in its 259 seat theatre on the campus of D'Youville College. Artistic Director David Lamb has taken the Kavinoky from its Anglo-Centric beginnings to a more broad based program that has even included musicals. The theatre continues to hold a reputation for quality productions.

New Phoenix Theatre
95 North Johnson Pkwy.
853-1334

This young theatre company produces five shows each season that focus on issues of significant concern to the gay community. The annual playwrights' competition is culminated by the staging of the winning submission. The season runs from September through June.

Paul Robeson Theatre
350 Masten Ave.
884-2013

Founded in 1968, as part of the African-American Cultural Center, Paul Robeson Theatre is dedicated to exposing the talents of African-American playwrights, producers, directors, actors and stage technicians. The season runs from September to May and consists of four or five productions and one children's show. Educational opportunities are available for all ages in every aspect of theatre arts.

Shakespeare in Delaware Park
Delaware Park Casino
876-7430
mid-June-late August

One of the oldest free Shakespeare Festivals in the country, Shakespeare in Delaware Park presents two of the Bard's plays each summer. Founded in 1976, with an emphasis on teaching theater students, the festival still focuses on education by offering apprenticeships and training to students from grade school through college. In addition, a fall season at area venues, features one or two classic works.

Studio Arena Theatre
710 Main St.
856-5650

Studio Arena Theatre is Buffalo's major Equity House, with the area's largest subscriber base and operating budget. Over the last four decades, notable actors such as Kathy Bates, Glenn Close, Celeste Holm and Jon Voight have performed on the Studio's stage. The theatre produces as many as ten plays per season ranging from classic drama to world premieres. The Studio Theatre School founded in 1927, offers classes and workshops on every aspect of theatre production.

Summerfare Musical Theatre
Daemen College
4380 Main St.
Amherst
839-8540

On the campus of Daemen College, Summerfare Musical Theatre stages four musical productions per season. Artistic Director Randall Kramer stages musicals ranging from Rodgers and Hammerstein to Andrew Lloyd Webber. The season runs from September to June and all performances are in the intimate 110-seat theater.

Theatre of Youth Company
Franklin Street Theatre
282 Franklin St.
856-4410
☞**KIDS**

Artistic Director Meg Quinn heads the area's premier children's theatre. The intimate 150 seat theatre brings children into the drama. In addition to the six play season the theatre produces touring plays for in-school performances. The Theatre School offers classes to students ranging from pre-school to teens.

Ujima Theatre Company
Theaterloft
545 Elmwood Ave.
883-0380

Ujima Theatre Company is an ensemble group that is dedicated to exposing the works of African American artists. For over twenty years the company has presented works ranging from classics of the Western theater to popular and lesser known African American works to premieres, including works written by founder and Artistic Director Lorna C. Hill. The season runs from September through June.

PERFORMANCE HOUSES

Buffalo State College Performing Arts Center
Rockwell Hall 210
1300 Elmwood Ave.
878-3005

Rockwell Hall, on the Buffalo State Campus, is used for over two dozen performances, classes and workshops each season. The 856 seat theater is home to a variety of performances including concerts, dance, drama, film and guest speakers.

Pfeifer Theatre
681 Main St.
847-6461

The Pfeifer Theatre is home to various theater groups' productions. Formerly the home of the Studio Arena 's main stage, the 360 seat theater hosts the Arena's "Studio Too," performances that may be riskier than their regular schedule.

Shea's Performing Arts Center
646 Main St.
847-0850

Shea's, an ornate 1926 movie palace, now hosts Broadway touring shows.

UB Center for the Arts
State University of NY at Buffalo
North Campus, Amherst
645-2787

The second-largest arts facility in New York, this 250,000 square foot complex houses four theaters, a screening room and two art galleries. The 1,744 seat Mainstage hosts local and national theatrical productions, concerts, opera and dance. The intimate 400 seat Drama Theatre is home to productions mounted by the Department of Theatre and Dance as well as touring productions. The Black Box and Rehearsal Workshop Theatre provide a flexible space for more experimental works and multimedia shows. Films, lectures and readings are presented in the Screening Room. *(See also: Galleries, Non-Profit)*.

Day Trips

DAY TRIPS AND BEYOND

NIAGARA FALLS

One of the most spectacular and renowned natural wonders on the continent, Niagara Falls is a popular destination for tourists from around the world. The falls are divided into two parts by Goat Island. The American Falls on the northeast side is the smaller of the two cataracts at 1000 feet across with a drop of 167 feet. The Canadian falls, known as Horseshoe Falls, is an impressive 2,600 feet along its curve and plunges 162 feet. Over 350,000 tons of water crashes to the bottom every minute, sending out a billowing mist and continual roar. Upon visiting the site in 1882, Oscar Wilde first quipped, "It is the first disappointment in the married life of many Americans," but then, after taking a trip beneath the falls, he remarked, "The roar of the waters is like the roar when the mighty wave of democracy breaks on the shore where kings lie couched at ease."

The American side affords a close view of the power of the American and Bridal Veil Falls, while the best panoramic view of both cataracts is from Queen Victoria Park on the Canadian side.

NIAGARA FALLS, NEW YORK

Goat Island
By car: from 1st Street
By foot: from pedestrian bridge across Green Island
☞**KIDS**

Situated in the Niagara River, between the American and Horseshoe Falls, Goat Island is a good place to explore both falls. Walkways lead to Luna Island, where Bridal Veil Falls can be viewed and to Three Sisters Islands, which extend into the upper rapids.

Cave of the Winds
Goat Island
Memorial Day- Oct. 31
Daily
278-1730
☞**KIDS**

This tour has retained its name although the cave that once brought tourists to an opening behind Bridal Veil Falls collapsed in 1920. The tour now begins with an elevator descent 180 feet to the base of the falls which was named for its similarity to the train of a bride's veil. A series of wooden walkways lead to a remarkable display of the powerful force of this relatively small waterfall. Rain gear and footwear are provided.

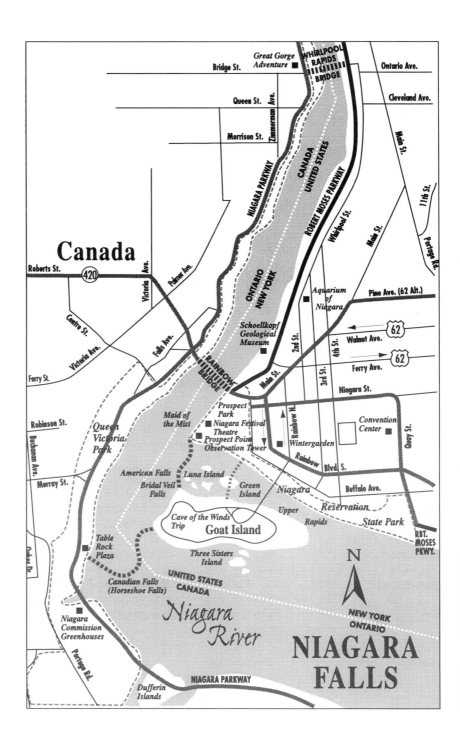

Aquarium of Niagara
701 Whirlpool St.
Daily
800-500-4609
☞KIDS

Aquarium of Niagara displays over 1500 aquatic animals representing nearly 200 species. The building is dominated by a two story 100,000 gallon sea lion exhibit. In addition, there are endangered Peruvian penguins, piranhas, sharks and a large collection of freshwater fish including many species found in the Great Lakes.

Maid of the Mist
April-October
Daily
284-8897 from US
(905)358-5781 from Can.
☞KIDS

One of the oldest tourist attractions in the world, the Maid of the Mist, has been ferrying passengers toward the falls since 1846. The coal-fired steamboat has been replaced by diesel-powered boats that depart approximately every 15 minutes from both sides of the river.

Niagara Power Project Visitors Center
4.5 Miles north of the Falls on US 104
May-Labor Day, Daily
285-3211 ext.6660
☞KIDS

The science of hydro-electric power is explained through the exhibits, short films, dioramas and hands-on displays at the Niagara Power Project Visitors Center. The observation deck, 350 feet above the Niagara River Gorge, provides expansive views and the fishing platform is a popular spot for anglers.

Castellani Art Museum
Niagara University
Niagara Falls, NY
Wed.-Sun.
286-8200

On the campus of Niagara University, Castellani Art Museum exhibits work from the 19th century to the present. The permanent collection includes works from Americans John Marin and Reginald Marsh; Europeans Raul Dufy, Georges Rouault, and J.M.W. Turner, and Hudson River School artist Albert Bierstadt. Changing exhibits include works focusing on Niagara Falls and regional artists.

Schoellkopf Geological Museum
.2 miles north of Rainbow Bridge
April-October
278-1780

This unusual building along the Niagara Gorge displays exhibits tracing the natural history of the Niagara Escarpment. A multi-screen presentation explores the 400 million year old formation and the Falls' development. The museum can be reached by foot along the gorge trail or from the pedestrian bridge from the Aquarium.

NIAGARA FALLS, CANADA

Queen Victoria Park
Niagara Parkway at the Falls

The best way to begin a tour of Niagara Falls from the Canadian side, is by walking along Queen Victoria Park. The park, established in 1885, is replete with floral displays and provides spectacular views of both the American and Horseshoe Falls. The Falls are illuminated nightly and firework displays take place Fridays from May to December.

Journey Behind the Falls
Table Rock House Plaza Niagara Pkwy. at Horseshoe Falls
Daily
(905) 354-1551
➡**KIDS**

From the Table Rock House, this tour begins with an elevator ride that drops 150 feet through the rock of the gorge to a series of tunnels. Two of the tunnels lead to openings behind the roaring Horseshoe Falls. The main tunnel opens to an observation deck that is remarkably close to the cascading water.

Great Gorge Adventure
Niagara Parkway, north of Whirlpool Rapids Bridge
Late April-Mid Oct.
Daily

The awe-inspiring power of the Whirlpool Rapids is best viewed from the boardwalk of the Great Gorge Adventure. The boardwalk proceeds along the Niagara River's edge providing views of the rushing water that moves up to 22mph as it drops 52 feet in less than one mile. An informational room at the tours' start chronicles

(905) 374-1221
☞**KIDS**

a facinating history of the tightrope walkers, swimmers, boaters and barrel travelers who tried to negotiate the rapids.

Niagara Spanish Aero Car

Niagara Pkwy., 3 miles downriver from the Falls
Mid-March-Nov., *Daily*
(905) 354-5711
☞**KIDS**

This cable car, operating since 1910, spans the Gorge 250 feet above the Niagara Whirlpool. Designed and built by Spaniard Leonardo Torres Quevedo, the car is the only one of its kind in existence.

Maid of the Mist

(905) 357-7384

The famous boat tour departs from both the U.S. and Canadian sides. *(See: Niagara Falls, N.Y.)*

Niagara Parks Botanical Gardens and Butterfly Conservatory

2565 Niagara Parkway
9 km. north of the Horseshoe Falls.
Daily
(905) 356-8554
or (905) 358-0025
☞**KIDS**

The Niagara Parks Botanical Gardens are part of the School of Horticulture, which provides classroom education and hands-on experience for its students. Since 1936, the students have cared for the 100 acre gardens and grounds that display a large variety of plantings. The rose garden alone contains 2,300 varieties.

On the grounds of the Botanical Gardens is the glass-domed Butterfly Conservatory. Over 2,000 butterflies representing more than 50 species flutter freely among the tropical plants, waterfalls and visitors. A glass display case provides viewing of the pupae stage.

Casino Niagara

5705 Falls Ave.
Daily, 24 hours
(888) 946-3255

One of the more popular attractions in Niagara Falls, the multi-leveled casino offers slots, video card games and gaming tables.

SOUTHERN ONTARIO, CANADA

The Stratford Festival
Ontario, Canada 90
miles west of Toronto.
May-Oct.
Information:
(519) 271-4040

Performing Shakespeare in a rural Canadian community was the bold idea of journalist Tom Patterson who in 1952 brought together Alec Guinness and Irene Worth for a production of Richard III directed by Tyrone Guthrie. Today, The Stratford Festival is considered by many to be the finest theater in North America. The festival no longer needs to bring in established British actors to draw sell-out audiences to its three theaters. The company has produced a number of its own talented artists including Nicholas Pennell and Brian Bedford. Just as in Will's birthplace, the Avon River winds its way through the quaint town. The season runs from May to October and in addition to works written by Shakespeare, the festival includes musicals, classics and new works.

NIAGARA RIVER REGION

Artpark
Lewiston, NY
Performances July-
August, Tues.-Sun.
(800) 659-7275

Artpark is the only state park in the nation devoted to the visual and performing arts. The 200-acre park along the Niagara Gorge, offers workshops, performances and demonstrations on the creative process from pottery to puppetry. The 2,300 seat amphitheater and the year-round Artpark at the Church, provide venues for concerts, plays and public events.

Herschell Carrousel Factory Museum
180 Thompson St.
North Tonawanda, NY
May-June, Wed.-Sun.

It was at this North Tonawanda factory where Allan Herschell, the best known carrousel maker in the US, first produced the popular amusement ride. Operated by the Carrousel Society of the Niagara Frontier, the Herschell Carrousel

July-Aug., Daily
Sept.- Nov., Wed.-Sun.
693-1885
KIDS

Factory Museum, chronicles the history of the company from inside the restored 1915 building. Several examples of carved animals are on display along with equipment and photographs relating to the fabrication of carrousels and band organs. Admission includes a ride on the 1916 #1 Special Carrousel, one of the first produced by the company.

Lockport Cave & Underground Boat Ride
21 Main St.
Lockport, NY
May-Sept.
Daily
438-0174
KIDS

One of the more unique tours that one is likely to find in the United States or elsewhere, is in the town of Lockport, NY. The tour begins with a hike up through a 30 foot diameter pipe, which leads not to a cave, as the name suggests, but a 2,430 foot man-made tunnel. The tunnel was the idea of Birdsill Holly, who began the project in 1858 to create a pumping system for the town's fire protection. Once inside, tourists board a boat and are motored down the tunnel where both the human history of the tunnel and the geologic formations are explained by the guide. In October, the cave turns into the creepy Lockport Haunted Cave.

Lockport Locks and Erie Canal Cruises
210-228 Market St.
Lockport, NY
May-November
Daily
(800) 378-0352

Lockport is known as "The Lock City" because of two sets of five locks each that once carried boats up and down the elevation change. This two hour boat tour passes through locks 34 and 35, which replaced one set of the five locks in 1918. The other set can be seen as five waterfalls dropping a total of 49 feet.

Old Fort Niagara
Fort Niagara State Park
Youngstown, NY
Daily
745-7611
KIDS

The strategically vital land that overlooks Lake Ontario at the mouth of the Niagara River, was first used as a fort by LaSalle in 1678. During the 18th century, the Fort was held by the French, the British, and by 1796, the Americans. The British recaptured the Fort during the war of 1812 before the Treaty of Ghent returned it to America in 1815. The oldest building on the grounds is the "French Castle," a fortress built in 1726. Most of the other buildings of the Fort were built between 1726 and 1872 and include a bakery, a provisions storehouse and a powder magazine. During the summer months, there are musket and cannon firings, demonstrations, and infantry drills.

Shaw Festival
Niagara-On-The-Lake
Ontario, Canada.
(800) 511-7429

Niagara-On-The-Lake is a picturesque 19th century village that is home to the only theater in the world that specializes in the works of George Bernard Shaw and his contemporaries. What began with weekend performances in a courthouse in 1962, now consists of three theaters and the second largest repertory company in the world. The ten to twelve play season runs from April to October.

GOING SOUTH

Allegany State Park
Salamanca, NY
354-9121
☞KIDS

The 65,000 acres of Allegany State Park offer a wide variety of recreational opportunities during every season. Warm weather activities take place on the beaches, lakes, ballfields, tennis courts, playgrounds and hiking trails. Trails are available for hiking, horseback riding and mountain biking. Non-motorized boats, bicycles and mountain bikes can be rented. The park features 315 campsites and over 380 rentable cabins, 150 of which are winterized. For winter recreation there are snowmobile trails, cross county ski trails and rentals, ice fishing and dogsled races.

**Chautauqua
Institution**
*Chautauqua, NY
16 miles northwest of
Jamestown
late June-Aug.
(800) 836-2787*

Chautauqua Institution, on the scenic shores of Chautauqua Lake, is a pristine Victorian village that began in 1874 as an summer encampment for Methodist Sunday school teachers. The birthplace of what is now called "continuing education," the Institution soon broadened its scope to include other denominations, and by the end of the century, "chautauquas" were a national movement. Today, the original Chautauqua, remains a center of learning, offering classes in a wide array of subjects. In addition, the annual program includes performances of music, theater, dance and opera. The quaint village with its picture postcard houses and its streets closed to vehicles, may be best known for its morning lecture series, one of the oldest and most important forums for open discussion in the country. Lecturers in the historic 5,500 seat amphitheater have included Alexander Graham Bell, Amelia Earhart, William Jennings Bryan and nine presidents. One speaker, historian David McCullough said of Chautauqua: "It has its own mythic force...there is no place like it; no resort, no spa, not anywhere else in the country, or anywhere else in the world."

**Millard Fillmore
Cottage**
*24 Shearer Ave.
East Aurora
June 1-Oct. 15
Wed., Sat. & Sun.
652-3280*

The small, wood-framed house that was moved to this site from Main Street, is the only home in the U.S. actually built by a president. Millard Fillmore practiced law in East Aurora for seven years before moving to Buffalo and eventually, upon the death of Zachary Taylor, becoming the 13th president of the United States. The house is furnished with items belonging to the Fillmores and period pieces.

☞**NEARBY:**   *Restaurants: The Roycroft Inn, Old Orchard Inn.*

**The Original
American Kazoo
Company**
8703 South Main St.
Eden, NY
Daily
992-3960
☞**KIDS**

This factory museum in the town of Eden contains everything you always wanted to know about this all-American musical instrument. The only metal kazoo company in the world is not just a working monument to the kazoo, but a fascinating insight into early 20th century manufacturing. Self-guided tours take place in the factory where kazoos are made the same way and with the same machinery as they were in 1916. Overhead, wooden pulley wheels dating from 1907, turn the leather belts that operate the die presses. Displays chronicling the history of the kazoo and amusing trivia keep the tour interesting. Make your own kazoo or purchase one in the gift shop.

Panama Rocks
11 Rock Hill Rd. (Rte. 10)
Panama, NY
May-Oct.
Daily
782-2845
☞**KIDS**

Pushed-up by glaciers approximately 165 million years ago, the giant boulders that make up Panama Rocks were once sea islands from the Paleozoic Era (~300 million years ago). A walking trail loops around the rocks and allows access to the crevices and narrow caves. Close inspection of the rocks reveals embedded stones, rounded from the waves of ancient beaches. The human history of the area is believed to have begun with the stone age, before the Eries and Iroquois used the rocks for shelter. In the 1800's, the rocks had gained notoriety for being the depository of bandits' loot as well as a hideout for counterfeiters' equipment and contraband. The Panama Rocks Folk Fair is an Early American festival that takes place the second weekend of July.

**Pedaling History
Bicycle Museum**
3943 N. Buffalo Rd.
Orchard Park, NY
Daily

The largest and most complete all-bicycle museum in America, Pedaling History Bicycle Museum contains over 300 rare and unique bicycles, along with cycling accessories and memorabilia. Examples include early pedal-less

662-3853
☞**KIDS**

models, wooden highwheels, military bikes and a 1913 bicycle still packed in its original crate. Also on display is the world's only marine "catamaran" bicycle, a 22' floating contrivance from 1881. The knowledgeable owners make the tour interesting as well as educational.

☞**NEARBY:** *Restaurant: Eckl's.*

Roycroft Campus & Hubbard Museum
East Aurora, NY
Roycroft Campus
Main & South Grove Sts.
Sat. & Sun.
Hubbard Museum
363 Oakwood Ave.
June-Oct.
Wed., Sat. & Sun.
652-4735

Roycroft, an Arts and Crafts colony, was founded in East Aurora in 1895 by former soap salesman, writer, and lecturer Elbert Hubbard. Hubbard drew much of his philosophy from the British aesthetic that viewed 19th Century industrialization as a threat to artistic expression and quality. From the campus on Main Street, the Roycrofters produced furniture, books, copperware, and leather crafts with an emphasis on quality. Nearby, the craftsman bungalow home of former Roycrofter George ScheideMantel, has become a museum showcasing a large collection of original works.

☞**NEARBY:** *Restaurant: The Old Orchard Inn, The Roycroft Inn.*

Toy Town Museum
636 Girard Ave.
East Aurora, NY
Mon.-Sat.
687-5151
☞**KIDS**

The Toy Town Museum, on the Fisher-Price Campus, was founded in 1987 as a non-profit organization devoted to preserving the history of toys. The Museum's collection includes early Fisher-Price toys along with original design artwork. Toyworks is a hands-on educational experience designed for children. The Museum also operates the popular Toyfest during the last week of August.

☞**NEARBY:** *Restaurants: The Old Orchard Inn, The Roycroft Inn.*

HEADING EAST

Clarence Antique Markets
Main St.
Clarence, NY
(800) 959-0714
(800) 343-5399

Clarence, the oldest township in Erie county (est. 1808), has several shops dealing in antiques and collectibles. The two largest, Antique World and Kelly's, constitute the state's largest antique market. Sundays have the most vendors. The biannual shows in May and August attract over 800 dealers from the US and Canada.

Six Flags, Darien Lake Theme Park
9993 Allegheny Rd.
Darien Center, NY
Mid-May through Oct.
599-4641
☞**KIDS**

Located between Buffalo and Rochester, this amusement park has over 100 rides and attractions, including five roller coasters, and a water park. The amphitheatre stages a summer concert series. Lodging and campsites are available.

Genesee Country Museum
1410 Flint Hill Road,
Mumford, NY
May-Oct.
Tues.-Sun.
538-6822
☞**KIDS**

The Genesee Country Museum is a 19th Century village that was created by moving 57 buildings from various towns and villages around upstate New York to this site. The carefully restored structures include shops, schools, churches and homes. Wander the streets, stopping to observe printers, tinsmiths, coopers, potters and blacksmiths demonstrate their crafts. There's also a nature center with five miles of trails and the Gallery of Sporting Art which displays hundreds of paintings and sculptures depicting hunting and wildlife subjects.

Letchworth State Park
Route 36 at Mt. Morris or
Route 19 A at Castile
493-2611
☞**KIDS**

Often referred to as "the Grand Canyon of the East," Letchworth State Park is comprised of over 14,000 acres of parkland. The Genesee River stretches through the spectacular 600 foot gorge for 17 miles and plunges over three waterfalls. There are forty-two miles of hiking trails, 280 campsites, several cabins, playgrounds and pools. Local balloon excursion companies can arrange a trip high above the gorge. In October, the Arts Festival draws large crowds. The nearby Glen Iris Inn is a popular restaurant built in 1914.

THE FINGER LAKES REGION

Take a drive east and discover the rolling hills, beautiful lakes and quiet towns that make up the Finger Lakes region. Travel the scenic routes that afford lake views like Route 89 along Cayuga or Route 14 on the western shore of Seneca. Along the way you may want explore the picturesque towns of Hammondsport, Penn Yan and Naples. Ithaca, home of Cornell and Ithaca College is worth a stop for its diverse shops and restaurants. North of Ithaca on Route 89 in Taughannock Falls State Park is the 215 foot Taughannock Falls. For more waterfalls climb the stone steps through Watkins Glen State Park where the 1.5 mile trail passes 18 waterfalls. Besides the natural beauty of the region, one of the best reasons to visit the Finger Lakes is to tour some of the wineries. New York State is the second largest wine producer in the US and over 900,000 tourists visit New York wineries every year. The following guide will help you explore the Finger Lakes wine region.

FINGER LAKES WINERIES

The glacier-carved Finger Lakes, deep and narrow, provide the picturesque backdrop for nearly fifty wineries that produce 20 million gallons of wine annually. The history of the wine region began with native American grapes in the 1850's and later progressed to French hybrids like Seyval Blanc and Baco Noir. Today, vinifera varieties, the same vines that produce the world's finest wine, are yielding fruit for a new generation of New York State wines. It wasn't long ago that the "experts" were professing that vinifera wines would never grow in the harsh climate of the Finger Lakes, but in the 1950's Dr. Konstantin Frank defied this notion and planted vinifera for winemaker Charles Fournier at Gold Seal. Frank was certain that the varieties that grew in his native Ukraine could grow in western NY. The successful growth of Chardonnay,

Riesling, Pinot Noir and Merlot grapes are proof that Frank was right. The wines produced from these vines have earned national and international acclaim. The area now bottles some excellent Chardonnay and is considered to produce the best Riesling outside of Europe. Advances in viticulture are helping to create some quality red wines as well. Touring the wineries can be an informative, scenic and enjoyable way to spend a day or two.

When tasting remember to always have a designated driver.

ROCHESTER AREA AND CANANDAIGUA LAKE WINERIES

The lake is dominated by the area's largest winery, Canandaigua Wine Co., the third largest winery in the world and owners of Widmer's Wine Cellars Inc.

1. Thorpe Vineyard
8150 Chimney Heights Blvd.
Wolcott
(315) 594-2502

2. Casa Larga Vineyards
2287 Turk Hill Rd.
Fairport
223-4210

3. Eagle Crest Vineyards
7101 Vineyard Rd.
Conesus
346-2321

4. Arbor Hill Grapery
6416 Route 64
Naples
374-2406

5. Widmer's Wine Cellars
1 Lake Niagara Ln.
Naples
374-6311

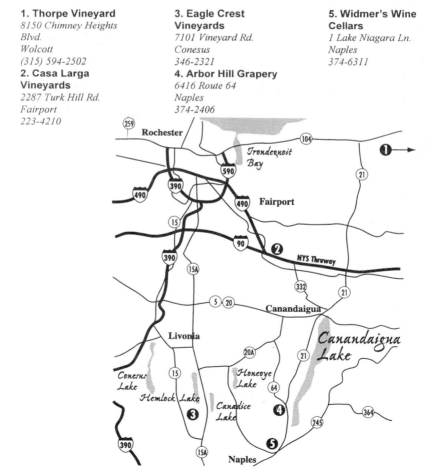

KEUKA LAKE WINERIES

The beautiful "Y" shaped Keuka Lake, is where the Finger lakes wine industry was born and where the "vinifera revolution" was started by Dr. Konstantin Frank.

1. Hunt Country Vineyards
4021 Italy Hill Rd.
Branchport
(315) 595-2812

2. Dr. Konstantin Frank's Vinifera Wine Cellars & Chateau Frank
9749 Middle Rd.
Hammondsport
(800) 320-0735

3. Heron Hill Vineyards
8203 Pleasant Valley Rd.
Hammondsport
(607) 868-4241

4. Bully Hill Vineyards
8843 G.H. Taylor Mem. Dr.
Hammondsport
(607) 868-3610

5. Pleasant Valley Wine Co.
Great Western Visitor's Center
8260 Pleasant Valley Rd.
Hammondsport
(607) 569-6111

6. McGregor Vineyard Winery
5503 Dutch St.
Dundee
(800) 272-0192

7. Keuka Overlook Wine Cellars
5777 Old Bath Rd.
Dundee
(607) 292-6877

8. Barrington Cellars
2772 Gray Rd.
Penn Yan
(315) 536-9686

9. Keuka Springs Vineyards
273 East Lake Rd.
Penn Yan
(315)536-3147

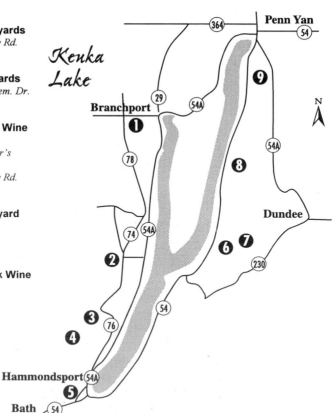

SENECA LAKE WINERIES

The wineries surrounding Seneca Lake produce some of the finest wines in the region. The depth of the lake helps moderate temperatures and the surrounding slopes provide good drainage. This trail begins on the west side of the lake, continues south until Watkins Glen, then moves north, up the east side.

1. Amberg Wine Cellars
2200 Rtes. 5&20
Flint 526-6742
2. Fox Run Vineyards
670 Rt. 14
Penn Yan (315) 536-4616
3. Anthony Road Wine Co
1225 Anthony Rd.
Penn Yan (315) 536-2182
4. Prejean Winery
2634 Route 14
Penn Yan (315) 536-7524
5. Four Chimneys Winery
211 Hall Rd.
Himrod (607) 243-7502
6. Hermann J. Wiemer Vineyard
Route 14
Dundee (800) 371-7971
7. Squaw Point Winery
Poplar Point Rd.
Dundee (607) 243-8602
8. Glenora Wine Cellars
5435 Route 14
Dundee (800) 243-5513
9. Fulkerson Winery
5576 Route 14
Dundee (607) 243-7883
10. Arcadian Estate Vineyards
4184 Route 14
Rock Stream (607) 535-2068
11. Lakewood Vineyards
4024 Route 14
Watkins Glen (607) 535-9252
12. Castel Grisch Estate Winery
3380 County Route 28
Watkins Glen (607) 535-9614
13. Cascata Winery
1006 N. Franklin St.
Watkins Glen
(607) 546-9302

14. Chateau LaFayette Reneau
5081 Route 414
Hector (607) 535-8000
15. Leidenfrost Vineyards
5677 Rt. 414
Hector (607) 546-6612
16. Finger Lakes Champagne House
5055 Route 414
Hector(607) 546-9463
17. Hazlitt 1852 Vineyards
5712 Route 414
Hector
(607) 546-9463
18. Standing Stone Vineyards
9934 Route 414
Valois
(607) 582-6051
19. Poplar Ridge Vineyards
9782 Route 414
Valois (607) 582-6421
20. Rasta Ranch
5882 Route 414
Valois
(607) 546-2974
21. Silver Thread Vineyard
1401 Caywood Rd.
Caywood
(607) 387-9282
22. Wagner Winery
9322 Route 414
Lodi (607) 582-6450
23. Lamoreaux Landing Wine Cellars
9224 Route 414
Lodi (607) 582-6011
24. New Land Vineyard
577 Lerch Rd.
Geneva (315) 585-9844

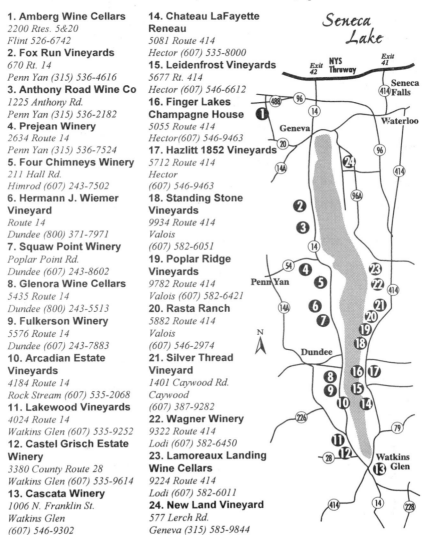

Seneca Lake

CAYUGA LAKE WINERIES

The wineries along Cayuga Lake are both smaller in number and in production than those of neighboring Seneca, but produce some fine wines.

1. Swedish Hill Vineyard
4565 Rt. 414
Romulus
(888)549-8326
2. Lakeshore Winery
5132 Route 89
Romulus
(315)549-7075
3. Knapp Vineyards
2770 County Road 128
Romulus
(607) 896-9271
4. Goose Watch Winery
5480 Rt. 89
Romulus
(315) 549-2599
5. Cayuga Ridge Estate Winery
6800 Route 89
Ovid
(800) 598-9463
6. Hosmer Winery
6999 Route 89
Ovid
(888) 467-9463
7. Sheldrake Point Vineyard & Cafe
7448 County Rd. 153
Ovid
(607) 532-9401
8. Lucas Vineyards
3862 County Road 150
Interlaken
(800) 682-9463
9. Americana Vineyards Winery
4367 East Covert Rd.
Interlaken
(607) 387-6801
10. Frontenac Point Vineyard
9501 Route 89
Trumansburg
(607) 387-9619

11. Six Mile Creek Vineyard
1553 Slaterville Rd.
Ithaca
(607) 272-9463

12. Signore Winery
153 White Church Rd.
Brooktondale
(607) 539-7935
13. King Ferry Winery
658 Lake Rd.
King Ferry
(800) 439-5271

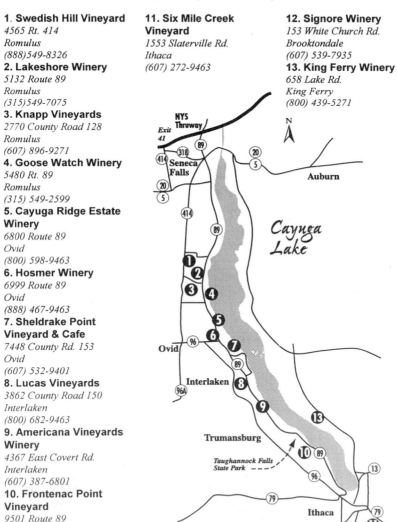

Calendar

JANUARY

Erie County Winter Carnival
Chestnut Ridge Park
Orchard Park
858-8355

Chestnut Ridge Park is the site of a wide array of winter activities including snowmobiling, sledding, skiing, snowshoeing and tobogganing on the last toboggan chutes in the state. There's also a woodsman's display that features log sawing, a pole climb and pulp-wood throw. For children there's kite flying, a casting competition, games and hay wagon rides.

FEBRUARY

Olmstead Winter Carnival
Delaware Park
851-5806

A four day event that includes a variety of winter events such as pond skating, sledding, cross-country skiing, ice sculpting, and speed skating. In addition, there are summer-type activities like softball and volleyball along with fireworks, casino gaming, a cocktail party, music and indoor and outdoor children's activities.

MARCH

Saint Patrick's Day Parade
Delaware Ave.
Downtown
875-0328

The annual parade takes place on Delaware between Niagara Square and North Street. Following the parade, the celebration continues with Irish food and dancing.

Winter Carnivals
Kissing Bridge
Glenwood, NY
800-367-9691
Holiday Valley
Ellicottville, NY
699-2345

Two of the region's ski areas host winter carnivals in March. Kissing Bridge has snowboarding competitions, a downhill obstacle course, log sawing and children's events. At Holiday Valley there's a cardboard box race, mountain biking on the slopes, and fireworks.

APRIL

Opening Day, Buffalo Bisons
North AmeriCare Park
275 Washington St.
846-2000

The triple A baseball Bisons open their season in one of the finest minor league stadiums in the country.

Opening Day Finger Lakes Race Track
Rte. 96, five miles north of Canandaigua.
427-7777/924-3232

Thoroughbred horse racing begins in early April and continues until December.

MAY

Greek Hellenic Festival
Hellenic Orthodox Church
1000 Delaware Ave.
882-9485/882-7121

Three days of celebrating Greek heritage, usually the third weekend in June. Traditional dancing, live music, and popular Greek dishes from souvlaki and spanakopita to pastries like baklava.

Thursday at the Square
Lafayette Square
856-3150

Thursday evenings from May through August, Lafayette Square is awash in music. All styles are represented and refreshments are available.

JUNE

Allentown Art Festival
Between W. Tupper and North Streets.
881-4269

Founded in 1957 by a group of Allentown residents, the Allentown Art Festival has become one of the country's largest and most respected art shows. Over 400,000 people visit the 450 vendors who are selected from approximately 700 applicants annually. Most of the proceeds from the festival are returned to the artists as prize awards or used to fund art scholarships.

Juneteenth Festival
Martin Luther King Park
Best & Fillmore Sts.

A celebration to mark the end of slavery, this festival features a parade, cultural dances, drumming, poetry, over 100 vendors, children's athletic events, and underground railroad tours.

Roycroft Summer Festival
Main Street
East Aurora, NY
457-3565

Home of the Roycrofters, (see: Daytrips), East Aurora is the site of this annual outdoor art show. In addition to the juried show, there's a craft show and sale, antiques and entertainment. The Roycroft Chamber Music Concerts run in conjunction with the festival at St. Matthias' Episcopal Church.

Shakespeare in Delaware Park
Delaware Park Casino
876-7430

One of the few free Shakespeare festivals in the country *(see: The Arts)*.

JULY

Waterfront Festival Summer Concert Series
LaSalle Park
884-8865

On most Tuesdays and Saturdays in July and August a series of free concerts is presented on the shores of Lake Erie.

Taste of Buffalo
Main St., between
Chippewa and South
Division St.
831-9376

The second largest event of its kind in the US, over 50 restaurants serve 150 taste-size specialties for between 50 cents and $3.00. Four stages of continuous entertainment and no admission charge.

Italian Heritage and Food Festival
Hertel Ave.
874-6133

Hertel Avenue, between Colvin and Delaware Avenues, becomes the site of Italian food, games, musical entertainment and rides.

Canal Fest of the Tonawandas
Tonawanda and North Tonawanda
692-3292

The Canal Fest takes place in two cities and across two counties. Water activities are prevalent and include: model boat races, water-skiing and jet-skiing demonstrations and hand-crafted canoe contests. There are also amusement rides and musical entertainment.

Blues Festival
Pearl St.
855-8800

The last Sunday of July brings blues and food to Pearl Street between Huron and Court Street downtown from noon to 10pm. The festival concludes with many of the local, regional and national musicians coming together for an open jam at the Lafayette Tap Room.

AUGUST

Erie County Fair and Expo
Hamburg Fairgrounds
Hamburg
649-3900

One of the largest county fairs in the country, the Erie County Fair features a wide variety of entertainment, exhibits, concerts, demonstrations, and concessions for 11 days in August.

Polish American Arts Festival
Cheektowaga Town Park
Cheektowaga
686-3465

A celebration of Polish culture begins with Friday's mass and ends with a fireworks display. In between there's ethnic music, dancing and of course, traditional Polish favorites like golmpki, kielbassa and pierogi.

Caribbean Festival
LaSalle Park
Downtown
881-3266

This two day festival presented by the Langston Hughes Institute begins with a parade that starts behind city hall and proceeds up Niagara Street to the park. At the park there's plenty of music, workshops, and children's activities, along with African and Caribbean food and goods.

Irish Festival
Bowen Rd. at Broadway
Lancaster
839-0002

A three day festival devoted to Irish culture. Irish goods, traditional music and dancing, activities for children, and plenty of corned beef and cabbage.

Scottish Festival
Amherst Museum
Tonawanda Creek Rd.
East Amherst
689-1440

Gain an appreciation of Scottish culture at the Amherst Museum's festival. Events include the pageantry of Massed Bands, Highland and Scottish country dance demonstrations, sheep herding with border collies, and storytelling. The athletic competitions include caber toss, sheaf toss and hammer throw.

Toyfest
Main St.
East Aurora
687-5151

A celebration of the heritage of toy making in Western NY. Events include a parade, an antique toy show and sale, an antique car show, a 10K race and lots of entertainment.

SEPTEMBER

Curtain Up!
Theatre District
Main St.
856-3150

The theatre season opens with this annual celebration on the third Friday of September. Prior to the performances, there's a black tie dinner and after the shows, the party spills out to street for music and entertainment.

OCTOBER

Salute to Autumn
Sprague Brook Park
Glenwood, NY
858-8355

This annual fall festival features over 200 crafters, kids games, a farmer's market and hay rides to view the foliage. There are also tours of the sawmill operation and maple sugar shanty.

World Pumpkin Weigh-Off
11199 Main St.
Clarence
759-2260

Family events, food, hayrides and huge pumpkins are some of the things you'll find during this 11 day festival in Clarence.

NOVEMBER

Viva Vivaldi
Area Churches
896-2515

Ars Nova Musicians Chamber Orchestra, presents a celebration of Vivaldi and other "vicarious visionaries" during the first four Sundays in November

Holiday Tree Lighting Ceremony
Fountain Plaza
Main St.
856-3150

The lighting of the 40 foot tree is followed by an array of family events including horse and buggy rides, skating with Santa and refreshments.

Festival of Lights
Niagara Falls, NY &
Ontario, Canada
285-8484

Both sides of the falls are illuminated with thousands of lights, Disney motion light displays, musical acts, fireworks and family activities.

DECEMBER

Santa's Park
Chestnut Ridge Park
Orchard Park, NY
858-8355

Chestnut Ridge Park is transformed into the North Pole for the holiday season. You'll find music and refreshments along with visits to Santa's post office and workshop.

First Night of Buffalo
Downtown
631-5731

Indoor sites all around downtown host a wide variety of entertainment that provides an alcohol-free way to ring in the New Year. Ball drop and fireworks at midnight.

WE BLEW IT!

Help make the next printing of **Buffalo's Best** even better. Are there places you feel we missed? Do some of our listings seem unworthy? Be a reporter and fill out the form below.

I feel_____

_____
(name and address of establishment)

deserves ❏   doesn't deserve ❏
to be mentioned in **Buffalo's Best** for the reasons described below:

Signed_____Date_____

I am in no way affiliated with the aforementioned establishment or its ownership.

Name_____

Address_____

_____Phone Number_____

Send to: Backhouse Press, P.O. Box 10873, Rochester, NY 14610
FAX: (716) 442-3908   **E-Mail:** backhousepress@juno.com